Search for Significance

YOUTH EDITION

Discussion Manual

By Dawson McAllister
and Robert S. McGee

Illustrated by Kim Trammell

Search For Significance—Youth Edition

Copyright © 1990 **Dawson McAllister**

Shepherd Catalog number 2075
Printed in the United States of America **ISBN 0-923417-12-5**

Editors: **Tim Altman and Wayne Peterson**
Art Direction, Design and Illustrations: **Kim Trammell/LoC Graphics**

SHEPHERD MINISTRIES
2221 Walnut Hill Lane ▪ Irving, Texas 75038-4410
Phone: (972) 580-8000 ▪ Fax: (972) 580-1FAX

Dawson McAllister

Dawson McAllister is one of America's outstanding youth communicators. He has been a youth pastor, coffee house counselor, author, TV host and friend to thousands of teenagers.

After academic study at Bethel College in Minnesota and Talbot Theological Seminary in California, Dawson became involved in a program for runaways and desperate teenagers that has developed into a nation-wide ministry. His practical experience and spiritual insight make him much in demand as a speaker at assemblies, weekend seminars, conferences and camps.

A series of prime time TV specials entitled "Kids in Crisis" has enabled him to provide spiritual counsel to teenage youth throughout the nation. Thirteen popular discussion manuals, ten video programs and a film series have multiplied his ministry to individuals and small groups.

With a heart full of compassion for kids and gifted with a magnetic personality, Dawson is committed to seeing that today's youth have a chance to hear the facts about how Jesus Christ changes lives.

Dawson lives with his wife and two sons on an historic farm outside of Nashville, Tennessee, where he enjoys breaking and training horses in his spare time.

Robert S. McGee

Robert S. McGee is a professional counselor and lecturer who has helped thousands of people experience the love and acceptance of Jesus Christ. He is also the Founder and President of *Rapha*, a nationally recognized health care organization that provides in-hospital and out patient care with a Christ-centered perspective for adults and adolescents suffering with psychiatric and substance abuse problems.

SEARCH FOR *Significance*

YOUTH·EDITION

CONTENTS

USE OF THIS MANUAL

SEARCH FOR SIGNIFICANCE is a study and discussion tool for individuals, one-on-one counseling, youth groups, weekend conferences, seminars and week-long camps.

SEARCH FOR SIGNIFICANCE is a teaching manual to challenge the thinking student who is looking for answers. It is an excellent resource for the youth leader who is seeking to develop the faith and commitment of students.

Scripture passages in this manual are highlighted to call attention to their importance and to make them stand out from the context. The Bible is our ultimate resource in life and is the heart of this study. Various versions are used to bring out the vital teaching of each passage and to communicate clearly what God says!

The questions are designed to motivate thoughtful discussion, make significant points clearly understandable and to apply Scripture to the individual in current experience.

The planned progression of this study makes it important for the youth leader and the student to follow the chapter topics in succession, at least for the first time.

Unit I Introduction

Is it just our society today, or have we always had a problem with liking and accepting ourselves? From the megadollars spent on hiding facial blemishes to the fear that we might not make the team, our attention is focused on the need to have what we don't possess, and be what we aren't. It seems that only if we could "have it all," that we might feel significant and sense our own self-worth.

History will demonstrate that almost from the beginning of time mankind has battled with that deep emotional need — that of feeling significant. Our first parents, Adam and Eve, were given some special privileges but they rejected God's provisions, and the effects still continue today.

Where can we find the self-esteem and self-worth for which we are longing? This manual will show how God through His love and forgiveness has made it possible for us to become truly significant. It will help us to understand the struggles students today are facing. It will also provide practical steps designed to lead us toward a new and richer sense of significance.

1 THE BIG SEARCH

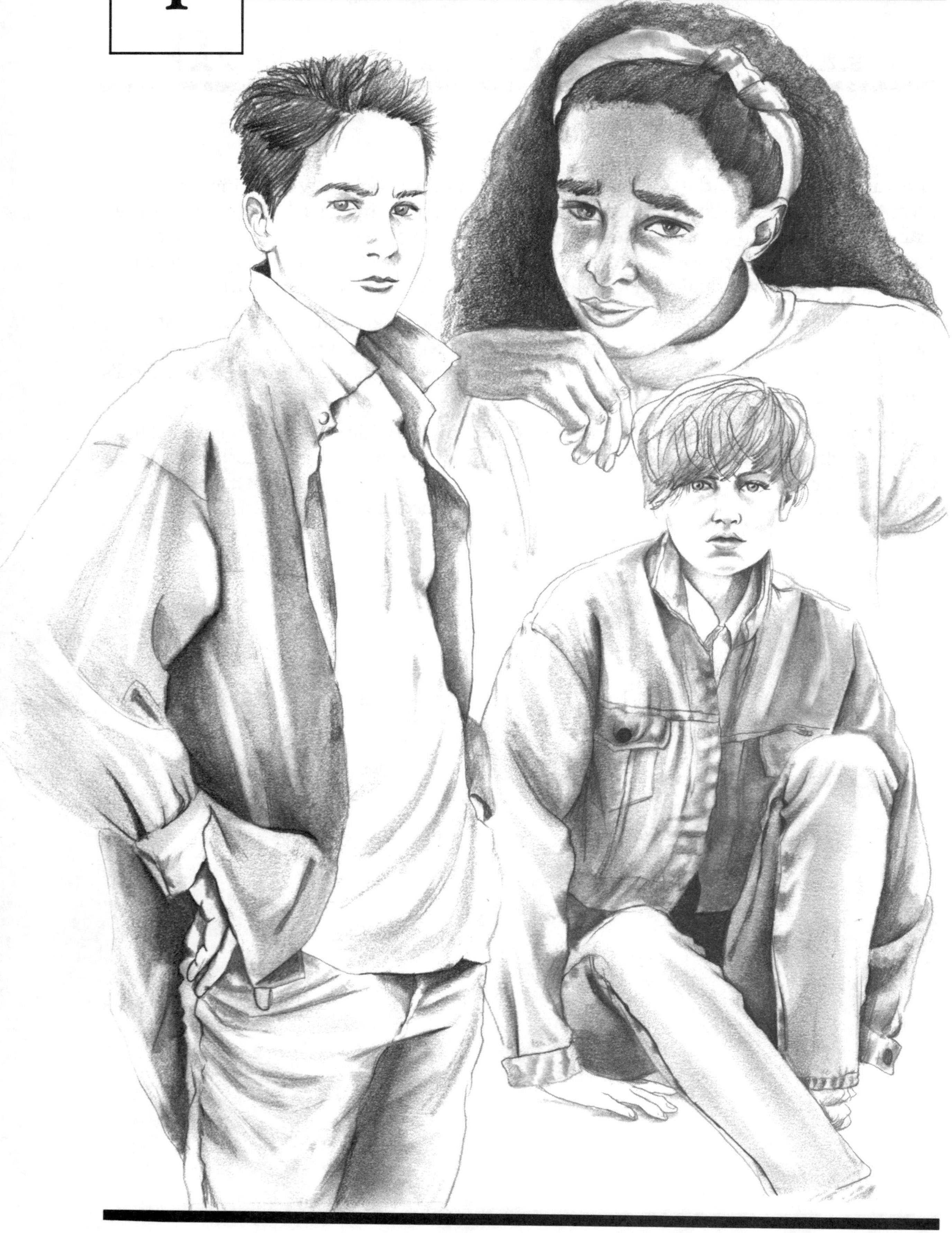

1 The Big Search...

Have you ever noticed how few people on your campus are really content or fulfilled? There seems to be a deep longing or craving inside most people for something more. For example:

- *Do you know someone who pretends to be like somebody else because he doesn't like himself?*

- *Have you ever known a person who has used drugs or alcohol to please his friends?*

- *Do you know anyone who's involved sexually only because he is looking for love and affection?*

- *Do you think there are students on your campus who work extra hard to achieve success through sports, popularity or grades, hoping that their success will make them feel better about themselves?*

Whether you know them or not, there are many people on your campus like those just described. They are constantly searching for ways to fill up the deep longings that seem to ache within them.

THE BIG SEARCH PROJECT

This project has five short paragraphs that discuss some of the incorrect ways in which students try to satisfy their deep longings.

Read these short paragraphs, then describe why you think each situation could create a problem.

Getting Good Grades . . .

Every student needs to do the best he can in order to learn and receive an education. However, some students base their entire self-worth on their ability to get good grades. These students are *"good grade slaves."*

Describe why basing your entire self-worth on getting good grades could create inward pain.

_____

_____

_____

Becoming Popular . . .

Everybody needs friends. It is neither emotionally nor spiritually wise to be a loner. Yet some students are so desperate to win the approval of others that they go overboard in trying to be popular. These students are basing their entire self-worth on which clique or social club they may be in at school. These "social scene fiends" are constantly struggling for more and more popularity.

Describe why basing your entire self-worth on being popular could create a sense of emptiness.

_____

_____

Having a Girlfriend or Boyfriend . . .

It's important to make friends and spend time with people of the opposite sex. There is so much we can learn from others' perspectives. However, some students look to these relationships to meet their deep inner needs. Sadly, these students do not feel loved or accepted unless they have a boyfriend or girlfriend.

Describe why basing your entire self-worth on your ability to have a boyfriend or girlfriend could create emotional pain.

_____

_____

_____

Owning Nice Things . . .

Almost everyone of us likes to own nice things (clothes, cars, compact discs, etc.). Unfortunately, some teenagers base their entire self-worth on how much they own. Because they regard these possessions as symbols of success, many students will: (1) work long hours to earn the money to buy them, (2) make demands of their parents, or (3) resort to stealing.

Describe why basing your entire self-worth on owning nice things could create problems.

_____

_____

Being a Good Athlete . . .

Playing sports is healthy and alot of fun. But, that can become too important. However, some students base their entire self-worth on how well they perform in a sporting event.

Describe why basing your entire self-worth on being a good athlete could be bad for your emotional health.

_____

_____

Discovering Our Deepest Emotional Need

Our accomplishments, whether in academics, possessions, or athletics, cannot bring us lasting satisfaction. Our relationships, no matter how popular we become, cannot provide the kind of love and acceptance our hearts are craving.

In fact, the Bible tells us that no matter how hard we try, or how much we pretend, our surface joys can end in pain and heartache if the deep longing within us is not satisfied.

> PROVERBS 14:13 (TLB)
> *Laughter cannot mask a heavy heart. When the laughter ends, the grief remains.*

Since our emotional and spiritual well-being is at stake, it is crucial to learn what this deep longing really is and how it can be satisfied. This longing, which we spend so much time and energy to meet, is our need for **SIGNIFICANCE** or **SELF-WORTH**.

What Does Significance Mean?

> **SIGNIFICANCE MEANS FULLY LOVING AND ACCEPTING YOURSELF BECAUSE YOU ARE COMPLETELY LOVED AND ACCEPTED BY GOD.**

A person who sees himself as significant will be able to say:

- *I am significant because God loves and accepts me.*

- *Because I have significance, I don't have to spend my life always trying to get people to like me.*

- *Because I have significance I can feel good about myself even when others don't approve.*

- *Because significance gives me tremendous self-worth I can feel good about myself even when I fail.*

- *Because I have a healthy self-esteem, I don't always have to have a boyfriend or girlfriend to feel like I'm O.K.*

- *Because God loves me unconditionally, I don't have to perform for Him to gain His love and acceptance.*

Unfortunately, gaining a sense of our own significance is a difficult struggle for nearly everyone. Most of us have the wrong idea about where our self-worth comes from. Therefore, from our early childhood we somehow reason we must do certain things and please certain people to feel good about ourselves.

Based upon what we have discussed so far, write a paragraph describing what self-worth means to you.

_____

_____

_____

_____

_____

_____

THE BIG SEARCH

The following is a list of questions to help you come to grips with your own sense of self-worth (significance). Take time to think about them and answer honestly.

	yes	no
1. Do you like yourself?	——	——
2. Are you glad you're who you are?	——	——
3. Do you genuinely love yourself?	——	——
4. Do you remain positive and confident even when you fail at something?	——	——
5. Do you take criticism without being angry or hurt?	——	——
6. Do you see yourself as a "together" person?	——	——

If you answered "no" to any of these questions, your sense of self-worth is lower than it ought to be. However, this is not surprising. Very few people in our world today have a healthy sense of significance. Fortunately, it does not have to remain this way.

God wants each of us to have a proper sense of significance. That is, He wants us to know that we are already completely loved and accepted by Him. Therefore, we should fully love and accept ourselves.

1 THE BIG SEARCH

The Source of Significance

The Bible tells us that learning to understand and accept God's unconditional love will make a huge difference in how we feel about ourselves. The Bible is clear about this when it says:

EPHESIANS 3:17-19 (TLB)

17) . . .*May your roots go down deep into the soil of God's marvelous love;*

18) *and may you be able to feel and understand, as all God's children should, how long, how wide, how deep, and how high His love really is;*

19) *and to experience this love for yourselves, though it is so great that you will never see the end of it or fully know or understand it. And so at last you will be filled up with God Himself.*

IN THIS MANUAL, WE WILL BE DISCUSSING HOW MAN HAS LOST HIS SENSE OF SIGNIFICANCE AND HOW GOD THROUGH HIS LOVE AND FORGIVENESS HAS MADE IT POSSIBLE FOR US TO BECOME TRULY SIGNIFICANT AGAIN.

IN CONCLUSION

Studying this manual will help you in three ways. First, it will help you better understand the struggles others around you may be facing. Second, it will help you to understand the painful struggles you're personally experiencing. And third, it will provide practical steps designed to lead you toward a new and richer sense of significance.

2

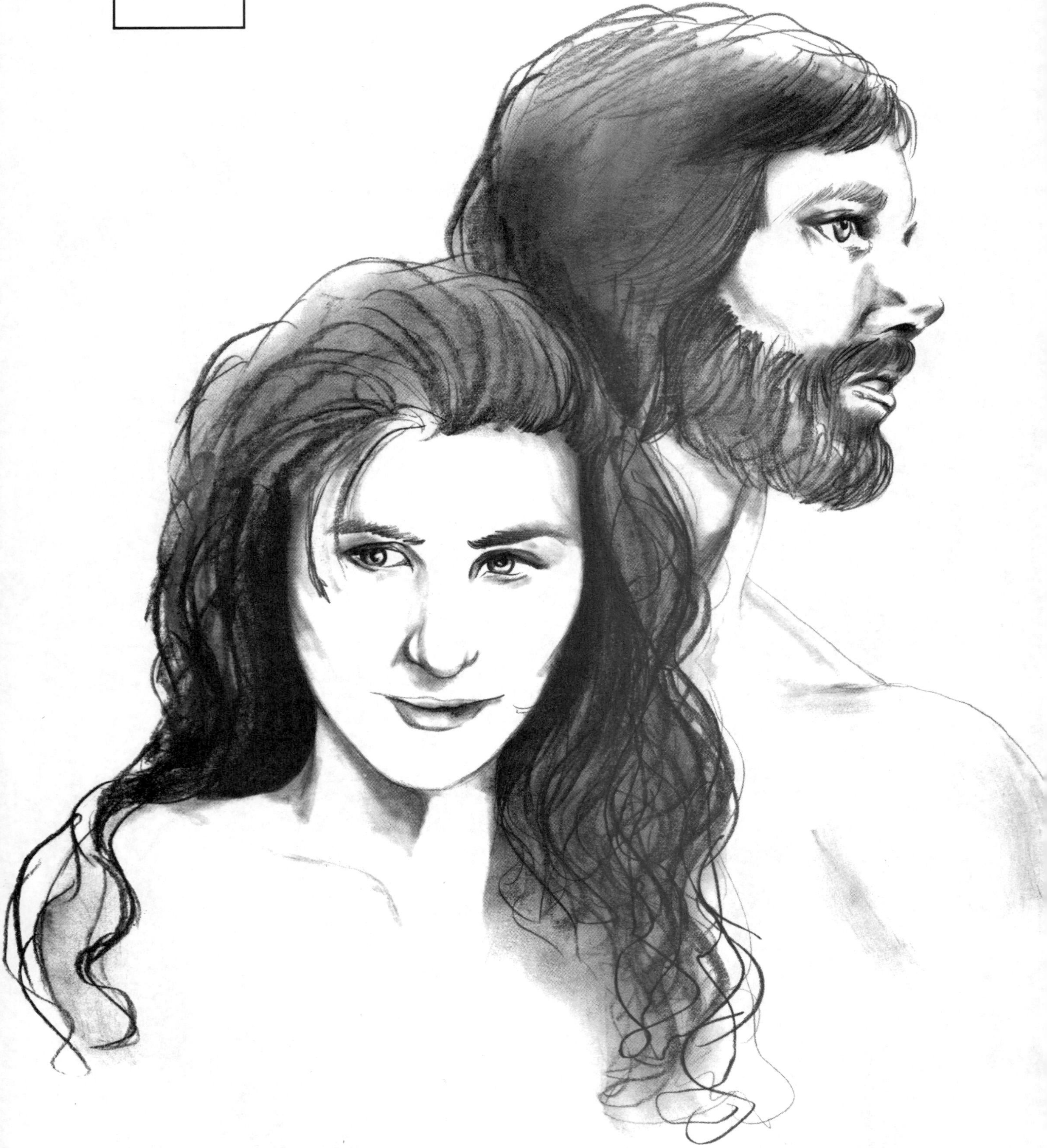

2 | Significance Gained and Lost...

When God created Adam and Eve, they were perfect in every way. They had perfect bodies and minds. They lived in a beautiful garden that provided everything they needed. Best of all, they had a perfect relationship with each other and with God.

God did everything to make sure that Adam and Eve would live a completely fulfilling life. They had a perfect sense of significance. Put another way, they fully loved and accepted themselves, because they knew they were completely loved and accepted by God.

Unfortunately, this perfect world did not last. They each made a tragically wrong decision that caused the loss of their sense of significance. In other words, they lost the ability to love and accept themselves. Instead, they began to experience guilt, shame, and fear. Worst of all, their failure, passed on to all mankind, continues to cause emotional and spiritual confusion for each of us today.

IN THIS CHAPTER, WE'LL DISCUSS HOW GOD GAVE ADAM AND EVE TREMENDOUS SELF-WORTH AND HOW THEY LOST IT.

2 SIGNIFICANCE GAINED AND LOST

A. Adam and Eve had tremendous self-worth because God created them in His own image and gave them important responsibilities.

The story of how God created Adam and Eve is one of the most amazing in the Bible. The following passage tells of the incredible way they began.

GENESIS 1:27-28 (NIV)

27) So God created man in his own image, in the image of God he created him; male and female he created them.

28) God blessed them and said to them, ''Be fruitful and increase in number; fill the earth and subdue it. Rule over the fish of the sea and the birds of the air and over every living creature that moves on the ground.''

What do you think the Bible means when it says Adam and Eve were created in God's image?

_____

_____

_____

You have probably heard the statement made that someone is the "spitting image" of his father. When a person says that, they mean that looking at the son reminds them of the father.

In the same way, God intended that everything about Adam and Eve would make it obvious that they belonged to Him. He gave them a complete personality modeled after His own. He gave them the capacity to think clearly, to feel deeply, and to make correct moral decisions. They were so wonderfully made that no one could ever question where they came from. God created them to be His image bearers, and the likeness was unmistakable.

To know that you were completely made in the image of God would be a tremendous source of self-worth. But God had even bigger plans for His image bearers.

2 SIGNIFICANCE GAINED AND LOST

In Genesis 1:28, the Bible tells us that God gave Adam and Eve two responsibilities. What were they?

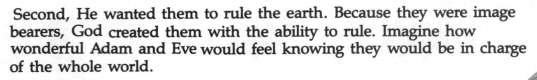

First, He wanted Adam and Eve to start a family. By doing this they would fill the earth and all history with image bearers like themselves. Their children would reflect the true glory of God. That is, all their thoughts, feelings, and actions would be pure and godly all the time.

Second, He wanted them to rule the earth. Because they were image bearers, God created them with the ability to rule. Imagine how wonderful Adam and Eve would feel knowing they would be in charge of the whole world.

In other words, God made Adam and Eve to be the king and queen of the earth. And their job was to create new "kings and queens" who would fill every corner of the world and rule it with love and justice and wisdom much like God Himself.

Not only were they God's image bearers, but they were His companion rulers as well. These honors were undoubtedly a tremendous source of personal significance for Adam and Eve.

According to Genesis 1:27-28, did Adam and Eve do anything to earn these honors, or the significance that came with them?

Therefore, would you say that God gave them their sense of significance as a gift?

_____

_____

God created Adam and Eve to have a deep sense of significance and to pass it on to all their descendants forever. It was an incredibly generous gift that they didn't have to earn or work for in any way. They didn't even have to ask for it. God wanted them to have it so they could live in perfect happiness and contentment throughout eternity.

B. Adam and Eve tragically lost their perfect self-worth because they rebelled against God.

To say Adam and Eve rebelled means they intentionally disobeyed God in an attempt to find significance and purpose apart from God.

> *Adam and Eve rebelled against God because they believed they could meet their own need for significance better than could God.*

The Bible tells us the story of Adam and Eve's rebellion in Genesis 3:1-6. In these six verses, God tells the tragic story of how Adam and Eve lost their perfect self-worth. Read this passage remembering that the serpent is actually Satan in disguise.

GENESIS 3:1-6 (NIV)

1) *Now the serpent was more crafty than any of the wild animals the Lord God had made. He said to the woman, "Did God really say, 'You must not eat from any tree in the garden'?"*

2) *The woman said to the serpent, "We may eat fruit from the trees in the garden,*

3) *but God did say, 'You must not eat fruit from the tree that is in the middle of the garden, and you must not touch it, or you will die.'*

4) *"You will not surely die," the serpent said to the woman.*

5) *"For God knows that when you eat of it your eyes will be opened, and you will be like God, knowing good and evil."*

6) *When the woman saw that the fruit of the tree was good for food and pleasing to the eye, and also desirable for gaining wisdom, she took some and ate it. She also gave some to her husband, who was with her, and he ate it.*

According to verses 2 and 3, Eve clearly understood God's command not to eat the fruit from that one special tree in the middle of the garden. Yet she did it anyway.

In verses 4 and 5, how did Satan tempt Eve to disobey God's command?

_____

_____

_____

First, Satan deliberately lied to Eve. He told her she would not die. Second, he implied that God was withholding from her something that would give her a greater sense of significance.

In verse 6, Adam and Eve both rebelled against God by eating the fruit. Explain why you think they disobeyed.

_____

_____

_____

2 | SIGNIFICANCE GAINED AND LOST

SIGNIFICANCE

When Eve ate the fruit, she proved that she was deceived by Satan's lie. That lie, simply stated, was that she could do a better job of meeting her need for significance than God could.

Adam, however, was not deceived by Satan's lie. He deliberately chose to forsake the love and security of God and follow Eve in rebellion. *(cf. I Timothy 2:14)*

Adam and Eve lost their perfect self-worth because they
rejected God's love and acceptance of them.

The Bible tells us in Genesis 3:7 that a terrible change came over Adam and Eve as soon as they disobeyed.

> **GENESIS 3:7 (TLB)**
> *And as they ate it, suddenly they became aware of their nakedness, and were embarrassed. So they strung fig leaves together to cover themselves . . .*

After they sinned against God, why do you think Adam and Eve suddenly felt embarrassed and ashamed?

_____

_____

_____

Unfortunately, when Adam and Eve disobeyed God, they suddenly realized that they were no longer trusting Him to meet all their needs. This made them feel inadequate and ashamed. Besides feeling inadequate and ashamed, they also became afraid to be seen by God.

In Genesis 3:8-10, we learn of the tragedy of their predicament.

> **GENESIS 3:8-10 (TLB)**
> 8) *That evening they heard the sound of the Lord God walking in the garden; and they hid themselves among the trees.*
> 9) *The Lord God called to Adam, "Why are you hiding?"*
> 10) *And Adam replied, "I heard you coming and didn't want you to see me naked. So I hid."*

Why do you think Adam and Eve hid from God?

_____

_____

_____

Based on what the Bible tells us in Genesis 3:8-10, how do you think Adam and Eve were feeling?

_____

_____

_____

Adam and Eve were feeling a whole variety of new and painful emotions. They felt guilt because they knew they had disobeyed God. They felt shame because they knew that what they had done was wrong. And they were afraid that once God found out, He would reject them completely. Therefore, they hid.

In summary, Adam and Eve lost their sense of significance. That is, they were no longer able to love and accept themselves, because they no longer felt loved and accepted by God.

IN CONCLUSION

Adam and Eve were the greatest achievement in God's creation. They were so much like God that anyone seeing them would immediately think of Him. They were completely perfect in every way. God wanted them to live a perfect life in the garden with Him and each other forever. They were successful, happy, and full of self-worth.

But, their perfect lives came crashing down because they stopped trusting in God to provide them with love and acceptance. Instead, they rebelled by trying to meet their needs without God's help. Adam and Eve lost their self-worth because the sin of rebellion separated them from God.

Adam and Eve, our very first ancestors, sinned against God and thereby passed rebellion on to all their descendants. This includes you and me.

Like Adam and Eve, we are also guilty of rebelling against God by not trusting Him to meet our need for love and acceptance. Because the sin of rebellion has separated us from God, we too have lost our sense of significance. This loss can only be replaced when we each accept a new relationship with God through Jesus Christ and believe that He meets these needs each day of our lives.

Unit II Introduction

God created Adam and Eve with tremendous self-worth. But they lost their self-worth when they rebelled against God. They wrongly believed that they could meet their need for significance better than God could do for them.

Today, we continue to have deep struggles over our self-worth. As with Adam and Eve, Satan has lied to us about where our true self-worth comes from.

As you recall, Satan played with Eve's mind. He deceived her into thinking wrong thoughts about God. He wanted her to believe his lie. That lie was that she could do a better job of meeting her needs than God.

Satan was not only successful with Eve, he has also been successful with us. We are deceived by the very same lie. Satan knows that when we believe his lies, we become separate from God's truth about our significance. This keeps us from having a true sense of self-worth.

Today, Satan uses many lies as he continues to deceive us. Most of his lies about our self-worth are summed up in these four false beliefs:

- *I must meet certain standards to feel good about myself.*
- *I must be approved (accepted) by certain people to accept myself.*
- *Those who fail are unworthy of love and deserve to be blamed and condemned.*
- *I am what I am. I cannot change. I am hopeless.*

God wants us to see clearly through Satan's lies about our significance. He also knows that for us to be able to do this, we must replace those lies with His truth.

In the next section of this manual, we'll not only be discussing Satan's lies about our self-worth, but also God's wonderfully freeing truth.

3 THE PERFORMANCE TRAP

3 The Performance Trap...

As he did for Adam and Eve, Satan, the father of lies, has many traps set for us to harm our self-worth. He wants us to neither love nor accept ourselves. His attack mainly zeros in on our beliefs. **Beliefs are deeply-held ideas that we perceive as true, existing both in our conscious and subconscious minds.** Because we all have fallen from God (Romans 3:23), it is difficult for us to think clearly and separate God's truth from Satan's lies. That is why the Bible says in Colossians 2:8 —

> COLOSSIANS 2:8 (NASV)
> *See to it that no one takes you captive through philosophy and empty deception, according to the tradition of men, according to the elementary principles of the world, rather than according to Christ.*

What do you think the verse means when it talks about being taken *"captive through philosophy and empty deception?"*

_____

_____

_____

When we are taken captive through philosophy and empty deception, it means we have become prisoners of dangerously wrong beliefs. These beliefs nearly always lead to wrong and harmful reactions.

What do you think "empty deception" means?

_____

_____

_____

Empty deception refers to false promises that we are tempted to believe but which can never come true.

One of Satan's most cunning deceptions has to do with what we'll call the Performance Trap.

IN THIS STUDY, WE'LL DISCUSS ONE OF SATAN'S MOST POWERFUL TRAPS — THE PERFORMANCE TRAP, AND GOD'S SOLUTION FOR FREEING US FROM ITS DESTRUCTIVE GRIP

I. What is the Performance Trap?

In the Performance Trap, Satan has made the false promise that success will bring us fulfillment and happiness. Deep down this lie promotes a destructive underlying belief. That belief is:

I must meet certain standards in order to feel good about myself.

A. Examples of being caught in the Performance Trap

Here are several examples of how students set standards of performance in order to feel good about themselves.

- *If I make cheerleading or drill team, I will feel good about myself.*
- *If I make good grades, I will feel good about myself.*
- *If I make first chair in the band, I will feel good about myself.*
- *If I make the varsity team, I will feel good about myself.*
- *If I lose weight, I will feel good about myself.*
- *If I make a lot of money, I will feel good about myself.*
- *If I'm elected to the student council, I will feel good about myself.*
- *If I'm accepted into a certain college, I will feel good about myself.*

The problem with needing to meet certain standards in order to feel good about ourselves is that no one can meet all the standards all the time. In our minds, the moment we fail to meet one or more of these standards, we sense we have failed.

Thinking we failed, we are left feeling miserable. Even if we succeed almost all the time, failure to meet our performance standards perfectly can be so devastating that we are left feeling like losers. Therefore, a person caught in the Performance Trap is a prisoner of the fear of failure.

Do you feel like you have to be successful in order to feel good about yourself?

_____

What things do you believe you need to succeed at in order to feel good about yourself?

_____

_____

_____

B. Symptoms of being caught in the Performance Trap:

Being caught in the Performance Trap creates a tremendous fear of failure. This fear leads people caught in the Performance Trap into behavior that can be painful and even dangerous.

The following list contains nine types of behavior that often takes place when there is a fear of failure. It is possible for some of these behaviors to be symptoms of other problems. However, if we can admit to ourselves that we have experienced one or more of these behavior symptoms, then we've already taken the first step to overcoming the destructive fear of failure caused by the Performance Trap.

1. *Perfectionism* — One of the most common symptoms of the fear of failure is perfectionism. The perfectionist cannot accept any kind of mistake or failure. If this is a problem we face, we will almost always focus our attention on the one thing that went wrong rather than feeling good about the things that went right. Perfectionists seem to be highly motivated, but the motivation comes from the fear that if we fail at anything, we will no longer feel good about ourselves.

2. *Avoidance of Risks* — Another symptom of the fear of failure is avoiding risks. Risk-avoiders are unwilling to be involved in anything at which they might not succeed. We may bypass new activities and potential friendships because the risk of failure seems too great.

3. *Anger and Resentment* — These symptoms may occur when we think our performance is being criticized. We may assume that criticism means that we have failed and that failure brings about a loss of self-esteem. Therefore, a person feels anger and resentment because he believes his critic is trying to steal the good feelings he has about himself.

4. *Pride* — A person caught in the Performance Trap may base his or her entire self-worth on being successful. Unfortunately, when this person achieves success, he also may become full of pride. However, the good feelings we experience as a result of pride seldom last long. They usually disappear at the first sign of failure. Pride looks like self-confidence but is really only a mask we wear to hide our fear of failure.

5. *Anxiety and Fear* — The stressful thoughts and feelings we experience when we think something in our lives might go wrong is anxiety. Anxiety, together with fear, often occurs when we are forced into a situation that we believe has a high risk of failure. The greater the chance of failure, the greater our anxiety and fear will be.

6. *Depression* — This is one of the most crippling symptoms of the fear of failure. If we fail more often than we think we should, we become convinced that we must be worthless. There are two common reactions to depression. A person may become passive, believing there is no hope for change, or he or she may become intensely angry at having failed so much.

7. *Dishonesty* — Dishonesty is an attempt to hide our failure. Most often we exaggerate the truth in order to take credit for things that will make us appear more successful. We also exaggerate to make circumstances or others seem responsible for our mistakes in order to avoid blame.

8. Low Motivation — Some people seem unwilling to become involved in any kind of activities. We may tend to believe that we lack skills to succeed at anything. Therefore, rather than face the pain of failure, we simply refuse to try.

9. Chemical Addiction — Many people attempt to ease the pain and fear of failure by using drugs and alcohol. Students who turn to drugs are almost always sending a signal that they are struggling from a lack of self-esteem. A chemical high does provide a moment of pleasure, and it seems to remove the pressure to perform. However, once the high is gone, the user can fall into despair, becoming more convinced than ever that he cannot cope with real life.

If you have experienced any of these nine symptoms then you are probably caught in the Performance Trap. Most likely your fear of failure is preventing you from enjoying a healthy sense of self-worth. In the next sections, we'll try to determine just how deep your fear of failure goes.

THE FEAR OF FAILURE TEST

The fear of failure is the result of the false belief that says, "I must meet certain standards in order to feel good about myself." How affected are you by this belief? In order to get some idea, take the following fear of failure test. But remember, in order for this to help you, you must be honest with yourself on each question.

Instructions

There are seven possible answers to each of the following statements. Read each statement, then choose the answer that is most true about you. Each answer has a number code beside it. Write the correct number code in the blank space provided next to each statement.

(1) Always   (4) Sometimes   (6) Very Seldom

(2) Very Often   (5) Seldom   (7) Never

(3) Often

NUMBER CODE

1. Because of fear, I often avoid participating in certain activities. _____

2. When I sense I might fail in some important area, I become nervous and anxious. _____

3. I get uptight. _____

4. I feel anxious for no real reason. _____

5. I am a perfectionist. _____

6. I feel like I have to defend my mistakes. _____

NUMBER
CODE

7. There are certain areas in which I feel I must succeed. _____

8. I become depressed when I fail. _____

9. I get angry at people who do things that make me look like I don't know what I'm doing or like I'm stupid. _____

10. I am critical of myself. _____

TOTAL (Add up the numbers you have placed in the blanks.)

Interpretation of Score

57 - 70 — This score suggests that you are virtually free from the fear of failure.

47 - 56 — This score suggests that you have a very small fear of failure. It may be that you feel this fear only in certain situations.

37 - 46 — This score suggests that you have a moderate to strong fear of failure. It is likely that a good number of your decisions are designed to minimize your chance of failing.

27 - 36 — This score suggests that you have a high fear of failure. Your emotional lows will almost always be a result of your fear of failure, or the belief that you have already failed in some way. Nearly all your decisions are designed to keep you as far from failing as possible.

0 - 26 — This score suggests that you have overwhelming fear of failure. Experiences of failure fill your memories. You are probably very depressed.

If you received a score that was lower than you'd like, don't panic. Nearly everyone has struggled with the fear of failure to some degree. But God does not want us to remain hurting and confused victims of the Performance Trap. The rest of this chapter will guide you through God's great solution for freeing you from this painful fear.

3 THE PERFORMANCE TRAP

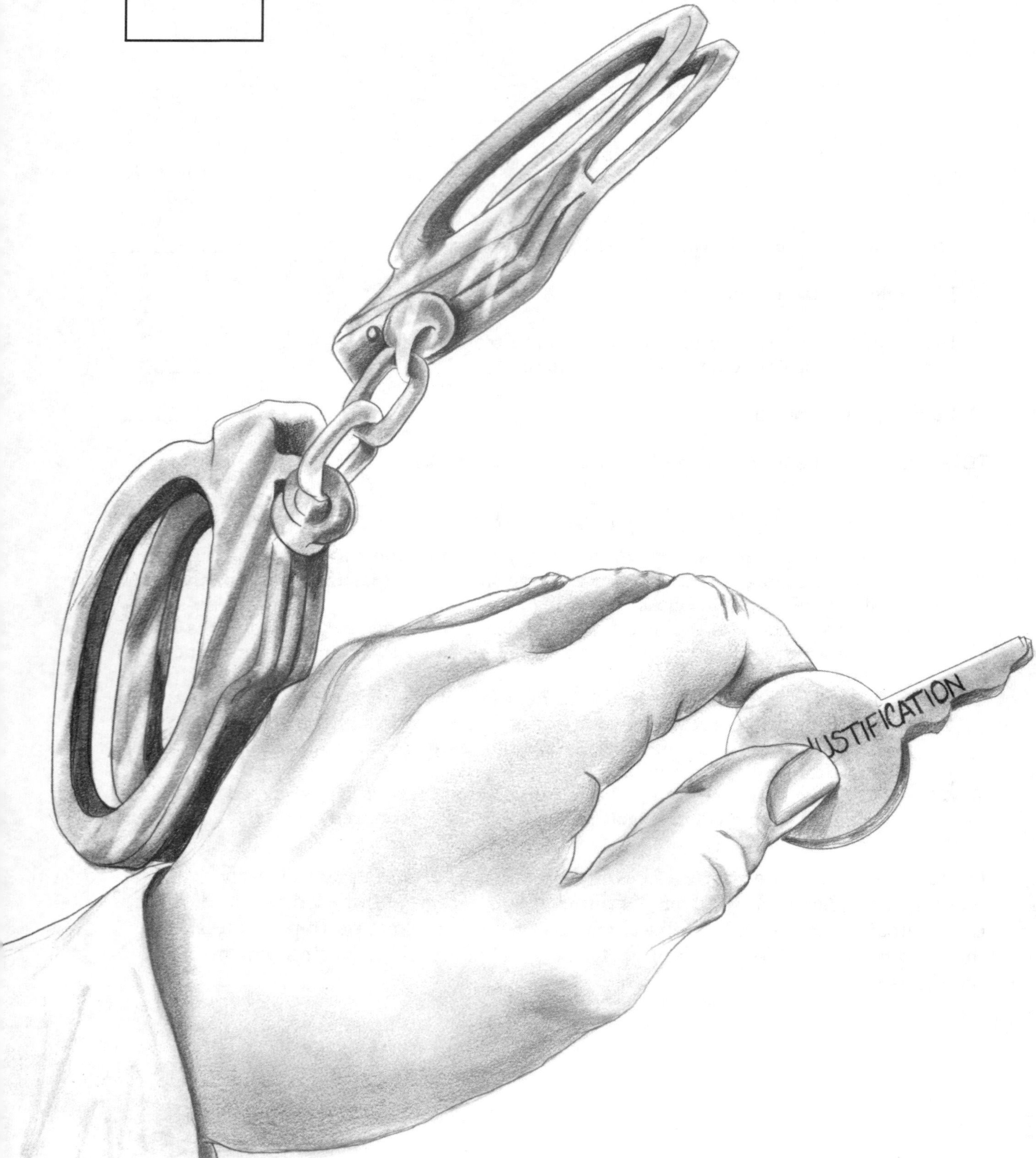

II. God's solution to the Performance Trap is for us to understand that in Christ we are completely justified and fully pleasing to Him.

A. What is Justification?

God clearly understands that because of our failures, we can never perform well enough to please even ourselves, let alone Him. The harder we try to reach perfection, the more we seem to fail. But because God loves us, He has worked through Christ to help us with our performance problem. Let's look at what the Bible says.

> ROMANS 5:1 (NIV)
> *Therefore, since we have been justified through faith, we have peace with God through our Lord Jesus Christ.*

In this verse, how does the Bible say we receive peace with God?

_____

_____

When Christ died on the cross, He paid the penalty for all our sins. This allowed God to forgive us completely for everything we have done wrong or even might do wrong in the future. But, amazingly, God has gone even further. Because we have believed in Christ and accepted what He has done for us, God has justified us. Justification means that God has declared us as righteous as His son Jesus Christ. In other words, when God looks at us, He sees us as completely pure and holy, without any faults. Therefore, because He looks at us as perfect, we will be able to spend all eternity with Him, and He will never change His mind about us.

The following series of drawings have been designed to help illustrate this very important Bible truth.

When Jesus went to the cross, he was perfect, clean, and holy. He had never sinned. In contrast, our lives were sinful, smudged, and grimy.

Christ allowed God to take all our sin away and put it all on Himself. Then He died on the cross in order to pay the penalty for that sin, so we would no longer be sinful, smudged, and grimy to God.

When Jesus rose from this horrible death, He was perfect, clean, and holy again. The Bible's word for this is righteousness. Christ now had an inexhaustible supply of righteousness with which He has forever covered us.

The Apostle Paul clearly states this truth in II Corinthians 5:21.

II CORINTHIANS 5:21 (NASV)
He made Him who knew no sin to be sin on our behalf, that we might become the righteousness of God in Him.

B. To be justified means we are also fully pleasing to God.

Since God has fully forgiven us for our sins and given us the inexhaustible righteousness of Christ forever, He will always be completely pleased with who we are — EVEN IF WE FAIL. This important truth about God's acceptance of us is discussed by the Apostle Paul in Colossians 1:22.

> COLOSSIANS 1:22 (TLB)
>
> *He has done this through the death on the cross of His own human body, and now as a result, Christ has brought you into the very presence of God, and you are standing before Him with nothing left against you — nothing left that He could even chide you for.*

Describe how you think God looked at you before your justification.

_____

_____

_____

What do you think the Bible means in verse 22 when it says that there is *"nothing left against you — nothing left that He (God) could chide you for"*?

_____

_____

_____

If you become the most successful person in history, you could not increase your worth to God. And if you fail miserably for the rest of your life you cannot decrease your worth to God. He has completely forgiven you for all your sins — past, present, and future. In fact, when God looks at you, He sees the righteousness of Christ. It is the most valuable item in the entire universe and it belongs to you.

Therefore, you no longer need to feel the fear of failure. You can be free of its painful and dangerous symptoms. God is as fully pleased with you as He is with His son Jesus Christ.

Because God has now completely justified us, you may be wondering why you shouldn't do whatever you want, even if it's sinful. Here are four good reasons:

First, God hates sin and it breaks His heart whenever we disobey.

Second, sin is destructive, and always has consequences that bring awful pain and heartache into our lives, as well as the lives of those around us. (Galatians 6:7 TLB)

Third, God will not punish us in eternity, but because He loves us He will discipline us in the present. (Hebrews 12:5-6 TLB)

And finally, Christ wants us to be so in love with Him that it keeps us from sinning. (II Corinthians 5:13-14 TLB)

IN CONCLUSION

As we have seen in this chapter, to some degree, most of us are probably caught in the Performance Trap. We have had the false belief that we must meet certain standards in order to feel good about ourselves. However, God has made it possible for Christians to escape this painful and often dangerous trap, through what the Bible calls Justification. Justification means that God, in His love, has totally forgiven our sins and completely covered us with the righteousness of Christ. Therefore, we are fully pleasing to Him in spite of our failures. Understanding this tremendous truth can help us finally to overcome the fear of failure.

THE CORRECTING-MY-BELIEFS PROJECT

Our beliefs have a tremendous impact on how we look at ourselves and on the things we do. As we have seen in previous chapters, God wants us to have the right beliefs about our self-esteem. He wants us to turn away from the wrong belief that says "I must do certain things in order to feel good about myself."

The following are four Bible verses that you can remove from your manual. Each verse represents a correct belief that will help you escape from the Performance Trap. Meditate on these cards each day until you memorize both the verses and the correct belief stated beneath it.

> **TITUS 3:4-5a (TLB)**
>
> *But when the time came for the kindness and love of God our Savior to appear, then He saved us — not because we were good enough to be saved, but because of His kindness and pity.*

Correct Belief — *I thank God that neither my success nor my failure had anything to do with Christ's love for me.*

> **II CORINTHIANS 5:21 (TLB)**
>
> *For God took the sinless Christ and poured into Him our sins. Then, in exchange, He poured God's goodness into us!*

Correct Belief — *I thank God that I am now as pure and righteous as His son Jesus Christ.*

> **HEBREWS 10:17 (NASV)**
>
> *And their sins and their lawless deeds I will remember no more.*

Correct Belief — *I thank God that I don't have to dwell on my past sins and failures since God has forgotten them.*

> **ROMANS 5:1 (TLB)**
>
> *So now, since we have been made right in God's sight by faith in His promises, we can have real peace with Him because of what Jesus Christ our Lord has done for us.*

Correct Belief — *I thank God that since He has declared me as pure and righteous as His son Jesus Christ, I am completely forgiven and fully pleasing to God.*

4 The Approval Trap...

As we have seen in the previous chapters, a lack of personal self-worth is one of the biggest problems facing mankind. Because of our rebellion, we tend to see ourselves as failures. Feeling like we've failed is at the root of our poor self-esteem. Yet for many of us, the problem is not only how we view ourselves, but also how we think others see us. Instead of basing our self-worth on God's love and approval, we tend to base it on what others think of us, and how we're accepted by them. Believing that our self-worth is based on what others think of us is a false belief that leads us to become addicted to their approval.

IN THIS STUDY, WE'LL DISCUSS THE NEGATIVE IMPACT OF THE APPROVAL TRAP AND GOD'S WONDERFUL SOLUTION FOR LIFTING US OUT OF IT.

I. What is the Approval Trap?

In the Approval Trap, Satan has made the false promise that the acceptance of others is the key to fulfillment and happiness. Deep down this lie promotes a destructive underlying belief. That belief is:

I must be approved by certain others to feel good about myself.

Or put another way, we say to others: "Please like me so I can like myself." "Please accept me so I can accept myself."

4 | THE APPROVAL TRAP

A. Examples of being caught in the Approval Trap:

Here are several examples of how students set standards of acceptance and approval by others in order to feel good about themselves.

- *In order to feel good about myself, I will only be seen with people who are popular.*

- *In order to feel good about myself, I will avoid those who I'm afraid will reject me.*

- *In order to win the approval of others, I will exaggerate the truth about my accomplishments or experiences.*

- *In order to win the approval of others, I will make sure I always wear just the right clothes.*

- *In order to win the approval of my boyfriend/girlfriend, I end up doing what they want me to do.*

- *In order to win the approval of my friends, I smoke, even though I know it is dangerous to my health.*

- *In order to win the approval of my friends, I do drugs, even though I know they may destroy my life.*

- *In order to win the approval of my friends, I try to avoid any kind of disagreements.*

You cannot guarantee that others will always accept you.

The problem with needing to be approved by others in order to feel good about ourselves is that no one can win that approval all the time. This is true because other people's moods, opinions, and circumstances are constantly changing. Nevertheless, we spend incredible amounts of time striving to please these people and win their respect. But, no matter how hard we try, one unkind word from the important people in our lives can seriously damage our sense of self-worth. It is amazing to see how quickly any kind of disapproval can collapse the self-assurance we have worked so hard to build up.

Have you ever worked hard at winning someone's approval only to feel like you've failed?

_____

_____

How did you feel when you were unable to win their approval?

_____

_____

_____

B. Symptoms of being caught in the Approval Trap:

1. Giving in to Peer Pressure.

One of the most powerful forces at work in your school is the awesome force of peer pressure. In the end, all of us give in to peer pressure in one area or another. While positive peer pressure is healthy, giving in to the wishes and whims of others just to be accepted is never truly satisfying, and can be destructive.

Sometimes giving in to peer pressure looks innocent. We may join clubs, play sports, or just try to fit in with a particular social group. However, deep down we are hoping that our actions will cause them to accept and approve of us.

Tragically, many students have admitted that their experimentation with drugs, sex, or even crime is a reaction to their need to belong. Though these things seem to promise a greater sense of self-worth, they can't provide it. Ultimately, life in the fast lane only leaves us with a deeper need for self-worth and acceptance.

All of us need to be loved and approved. But, when we become consumed with trying to earn that love and approval from our friends, we will always wind up disappointed and in pain.

Describe someone you know who has given in to peer pressure in hopes of being accepted.

_____

_____

_____

_____

In what areas do you feel the most peer pressure?

_____

_____

_____

Think back to a situation where you struggled with peer pressure. Describe how you handled it and why?

_____

_____

_____

As we have seen, giving in to peer pressure in order to gain approval doesn't work. At one time or another, about all of us have given in to peer pressure in order to gain approval. Unfortunately, it can never meet our true need for acceptance.

2. *The Inability to Give or Receive Love.*

One of the most painful symptoms of being caught in the Approval Trap is the inability to give or receive love. This symptom grows out of a desperate fear of rejection. Because we are so afraid of being rejected, we become unwilling to share our inner thoughts and feelings with others. Our fear has us terrified that others will reject us if they discover what we are really like on the inside. As a result, our lives tend to be marked by superficial relationships, or even isolation. The stronger our fear of rejection, the more unable we are to give or receive love. Thus, many students find themselves caught in the heartache of loneliness.

Why do you think so many students on your campus are lonely?

_____

_____

_____

Describe a time when you felt the most lonely.

_____

_____

_____

If someone wanted to overcome the inability to give and receive love, how would they do it?

_____

_____

_____

All of us need to give and receive love. If we don't, then we aren't spiritually and emotionally healthy. The fear of rejection is like a disease. The loneliness it creates for us will only get worse.

THE FEAR OF REJECTION TEST

The fear of rejection is the result of the false belief that says, "I must be approved by certain others to feel good about myself." How affected are you by this belief? In order to get some idea, take the fear of rejection test that follows. But remember, in order for this to help you, you must be honest with yourself on each question.

Instructions

There are seven possible answers to each of the following statements. Read each statement, then choose the answer that is most true about you. Each answer has a number code beside it. Write the correct number code in the blank space provided next to each statement.

(1) Always	(4) Sometimes	(6) Very Seldom
(2) Very Often	(5) Seldom	(7) Never
(3) Often		

NUMBER CODE

1. I avoid certain people. _____

2. I become nervous and anxious when I sense someone might reject me. _____

3. I am uncomfortable around those who are different from me. _____

4. It bothers me when someone is unfriendly to me. _____

5. I am basically shy and unsocial. _____

6. I am critical of others. _____

7. I find myself trying to impress others. _____

8. I become depressed when someone criticizes me. _____

9. I always try to figure out what people think of me. _____

10. I feel like people are always trying to manipulate me. _____

TOTAL (Add up the numbers you have placed in the blanks.) _____

Interpretation of Score

57 - 70 — This score indicates that you are virtually free from the fear of rejection.

47 - 56 — This score indicates that you have a very small fear of rejection. It may be that you feel this fear only in certain situations.

37 - 46 — This score indicates that you have a moderate to strong fear of rejection. It is likely that a good number of your decisions are designed to keep you as far from rejection as possible.

27 - 36 — This score indicates that you have a high fear of rejection. Your emotional lows will almost always be a result of your fear of rejection, or the belief that you have already been rejected. Nearly all your decisions are designed to keep you as far from rejection as possible.

0 - 26 — This score indicates that you have an overwhelming fear of rejection. Experiences of rejection fill your memories. You may be very depressed.

If you received a score that was lower than you'd like, don't panic. Nearly everyone has struggled with the fear of rejection. However, God does not want us to remain hurting and confused victims of the Approval Trap. The rest of this chapter will guide you through God's great solution for freeing you from this needless trap.

II. God's solution to the Approval Trap is for us to under-stand that in Christ we are reconciled to Him, and therefore, totally accepted.

The reason we suffer from the problems caused by the fear of rejection is that we have wrongly believed Satan's lie. That lie says that our self-worth depends on how well others accept us. We crave friendship and love, and we turn to others to meet these needs. However, the problem with basing our worth on the approval of others is that they often fail to meet our needs. Fortunately, God has a wonderful solution for meeting our need for approval. That solution is reconciliation.

A. What is reconciliation?

Reconciliation is a big word, but its meaning is simple. It means that those who were enemies have become friends. Spiritually, reconciliation means that although we were enemies of God, because of Christ, we are now His very closest friends. The Bible states this clearly.

COLOSSIANS 1:20-21 (TLB)

(20) It was through what his Son did that God cleared a path for everything to come to him . . . for Christ's death on the cross has made peace with God for all by his blood.

(21) This includes you who were once so far away from God. You were his enemies and hated him and were separated from him by your evil thoughts and actions, yet now he has brought you back as his friends.

According to verse 21 before we were reconciled to God, what was our relationship toward Him and how did we feel about Him?

_____

_____

_____

Before we were reconciled to God, how do you think He felt about us?

_____

_____

_____

According to verse 20 what did Jesus do to solve this horrible situation between God and us?

_____

_____

_____

Because of Christ's work on the cross, what kind of relationship can we now have with God?

_____

_____

_____

Reconciliation is more than Justification.

As we saw in the last chapter, God has already justified us. That is, He has declared us not guilty and covered us with the complete righteousness of Christ. But when He reconciled us, He went a step further. He has offered to be our closest friend.

Perhaps this short story will help you better understand reconciliation.

Let's suppose that you had received hundreds of traffic tickets and thousands of dollars worth of fines. Finally, you are arrested and brought before the judge. The judge is angry with you because you have not only broken the law, but you have not paid your fines. When he is finished, he pronounces you guilty and gives you a fine so big that it is impossible for you ever to pay. Just when you are feeling completely hopeless about your awful predicament, a man stands up and tells the judge that he wants to pay your fine. In fact, he wants to pay all your penalties and fines from this point onward. However, the judge needs your permission to accept his payment. Though you can't understand why this man is being so kind and generous, you accept. Immediately, the judge changes his whole attitude toward you. He comes down from his seat, puts his arm around you and invites you to become his best friend. You are thrilled, but confused. The judge then explains that the man who paid the fine was his son. And if his son thought enough of you to pay your fines, then he (the judge) wanted to stand by you and be your friend no matter what mistakes you might make in the future.

Obviously this story has been tremendously simplified in order to help you understand just how amazing God's friendship is. He has not only declared us not guilty and covered us with the righteousness of Christ (justification), but He has also committed Himself to be our closest friend forever (reconciliation), no matter what anyone else thinks of us. The Bible talks about this amazing friendship in Isaiah 57:15. Read this verse and then take a few minutes to think about what it means to be God's best friend.

ISAIAH 57:15 (TLB)

The high and lofty one who inhabits eternity, the Holy One, says this: I live in that high and holy place where those with contrite, humble spirits dwell; and I refresh the humble and give new courage to those with repentant hearts.

B. Because we are God's friends, we are always totally accepted by Him.

God became our friend because He wanted to have an ongoing relationship with us. He wanted us to learn more about Him and enjoy His friendship more each day. In fact, in Romans 5:10, the Bible tells that as God's friend, we have much to look forward to.

> ROMANS 5:10 (TLB)
> *And since, when we were His enemies, we were brought back to God by the death of His Son, what blessings He must have for us now that we are His friends, and He is living within us!*

Romans 5:10 says that part of the way God shows His friendship for us is by living within us. Why is that important?

_____

_____

_____

In what way has God shown His friendship to you?

_____

_____

_____

By saying that He lives within us, God wants us to know that He understands us completely. He will never be surprised or impatient with our problems or failures. He has totally accepted us just as we are. He stays with us day and night and never tires of loving and accepting us. It is true that we may have friends who love and care for us. Friends like that are a great gift from God. But only God Himself knows and loves us so completely that he can meet our needs perfectly.

Best of all, the Bible teaches us that God's love and friendship cannot be damaged and will never end. The Apostle Paul says:

ROMANS 8:38-39 (TLB)

For I am convinced that nothing can ever separate us from His love. Death can't, and life can't. The angels won't, and all the powers of hell itself cannot keep God's love away. Our fears for today, our worries about tomorrow, or where we are — high above the sky, or in the deepest ocean — nothing will ever be able to separate us from the love of God demonstrated by our Lord Jesus Christ when He died for us.

IN CONCLUSION

As we have seen in this chapter, to some degree, most of us are probably caught in the Approval Trap. We have had the false belief that we must be approved by certain others to feel good about ourselves. However, God has made it possible for Christians to escape this painful and often dangerous trap, through what the Bible calls Reconciliation. Reconciliation means that God, in His love, has become our closest friend. Therefore, we are totally approved and accepted by Him in spite of our failures.

We must remember that God still hates our sin and is deeply hurt by it. But, this pledge of friendship means that He will do everything possible to help us live happier, purer, more godly lives.

THE CORRECTING-MY-BELIEFS PROJECT

The following are four Bible verses that you can remove from your manual. Each verse represents a correct belief that will help you escape from the Approval Trap. Meditate on these each day until you memorize both the verses and the correct belief stated beneath it.

> COLOSSIANS 1:20-21 (TLB)
>
> 20) *It was through what his Son did that God cleared a path for everything to come to Him — all things in heaven and on earth — for Christ's death on the cross has made peace with God for all by His blood.*
>
> 21) *This includes you who were once so far away from God. You were His enemies and hated Him and were separated from Him by your evil thoughts and actions, yet now He has brought you back as His friends.*

<u>Correct Belief</u> — *I thank God that even though I was His enemy, He has now chosen me to be a very close friend.*

> ROMANS 5:10 (TLB)
>
> *And since, when we were His enemies, we were brought back to God by the death of His Son, what blessings He must have for us now that we are His friends, and He is living within us!*

<u>Correct Belief</u> — *I thank God that the Christ that lives inside me, knows everything about me and completely accepts me.*

ROMANS 8:38-39 (TLB)

For I am convinced that nothing can ever separate us from His love. Death can't, and life can't. The angels won't, and all the powers of hell itself cannot keep God's love away. Our fears for today, our worries about tomorrow, or where we are — high above the sky, or in the deepest ocean — nothing will ever be able to separate us from the love of God demonstrated by our Lord Jesus Christ when He died for us.

Correct Belief — *I thank God that no matter how I fail, I cannot keep Him from loving and accepting me.*

JOHN 15:15 (TLB)

I no longer call you slaves, for a master doesn't confide in his slaves; now you are my friends, proved by the fact that I have told you everything the Father told me.

Correct Belief — *I thank God that Jesus is showing His friendship for me by teaching me how to be godly and loving like Himself.*

5 The Blame Game Trap...

As we have seen in the last two chapters, Satan has set subtle, but deadly traps for us. These traps are designed to steal our self-esteem. When we fall into these traps, it is because Satan's lies have led us into wrong beliefs. Two of the most common wrong beliefs are:

1. *I must meet certain standards in order to feel good about myself.*
   (The Performance Trap)
2. *I must be approved by certain others in order to feel good about myself.*
   (The Approval Trap)

We tend to base our self-esteem on how well we measure up to these standards. The problem is that no matter how well we perform, or how much approval we gain, all of us will at some time fail. Because we believe that failure damages our self-esteem, we desperately look for some way to minimize our mistakes. All too often, our solution is to find someone to blame.

IN THIS CHAPTER, WE'LL DISCUSS ONE OF SATAN'S MOST RUTHLESS TRAPS — THE BLAME GAME TRAP — AND THE INCREDIBLE SACRIFICE GOD MADE TO DELIVER US FROM IT.

5 | THE BLAME GAME TRAP

I. What is the Blame Game Trap?

Nobody likes to fail. But the Blame Game Trap takes our fear of failure a dangerous step further. This false belief states that in order to protect our own self-worth, we can feel completely justified when we blame and condemn those who fail.

Simply stated, the Blame Game Trap represents the false belief that says:

> *Those who fail are unworthy of love and deserve to be punished.*

For most of us, finding someone to blame is almost automatic. We tend to blame our failures on others whenever possible. Sometimes because we find failure so unacceptable, we even condemn ourselves. In the end, it is not unusual for us to turn the blame on God, accusing Him of being unfair to us.

Describe a time when you blamed someone else for a mistake or failure. Include some of the things you said and the way you felt afterwards.

_____

_____

_____

_____

Describe a time when you blamed yourself for a mistake or failure. Try to describe your feelings.

_____

_____

_____

_____

Describe a time when you blamed God for a mistake or failure. Why did you think it was God's fault?

_____

_____

_____

_____

5 THE BLAME GAME TRAP

Examples of being caught in the Blame Game Trap:

Here is just a small list of things we might say to ourselves when handing out blame for things we perceive as failure.

- *I would have gotten a better biology grade, but my lab partner messed up too many of the experiments.*

- *If the coach would stop playing favorites with certain people, I'd get to play more.*

- *If my parents didn't have so many rules that keep me trapped at home, I'd have a lot more friends.*

- *I'd be making a lot more money by now if my boss didn't have it in for me.*

- *If I were better looking, I'd have more dates.*

- *I must really be stupid if I failed that last test.*

- *If God loved me, He wouldn't have let my parents get divorced.*

These are just a few of the hundreds of examples that we may use when we get caught in the Blame Game Trap. Let's now take a close look at how the Blame Game Trap works, and how it can damage our self-esteem.

A. We play the Blame Game by blaming others.

Problems in our relationships can cause tremendous emotional pain. All too often, we are the cause of this pain. We rush to blame someone each time we run into failure in our lives. Yet we seldom stop to think how our blame will damage our relationships.

Why do we blame others?

In order to be successful, we must often depend on the help of others. For example:

- To be a successful student, I depend on my teachers to be fair.
- To be a successful athlete:
  I depend on my coaches to make the right decisions.
  I depend on my teammates to play well.
- To be successful socially, I depend on my friends and others to accept me.
- To be a successful person, I depend on my parents:
  to not embarrass me.
  to not be too strict.
  to provide me with enough money and freedom.
  to love and accept me.

Obviously, we can't make it through life without depending on others. Unfortunately, the people we depend on frequently fail to live up to our expectations. When we perceive that our success is being threatened by their failure, we react by blaming them. Through blaming others, we hope to protect our fragile sense of self-worth.

The problem with this is that the constant blame we spread hoping to protect our own self-esteem almost always damages the self-esteem of others.

Describe a time when someone got in the way of your becoming successful. Explain how you became critical of them.

_____

_____

_____

_____

Another reason we blame others is to make ourselves feel better. This is especially true if the person we blame for failing is more popular than we are, or has some authority over us. Some of the people we blame most often include:

- *parents*
- *teachers*
- *coaches*
- *bosses*

- *team captains*
- *club officers*
- *student council members*
- *gifted classmates*

Heaping blame on people whom we think are superior to us in some way is actually an attempt to gain superiority for ourselves. Our reasoning goes like this — *"You seem to be better than me, but because you failed and I didn't, I must be superior to you."* This kind of thinking goes beyond protecting our own sense of self-worth. Now we are actively trying to tear down someone else in the false belief that it will actually improve our own self-worth.

Describe a time when you heard someone cut another person down in an attempt to improve their own sense of self-worth.

_____

_____

_____

_____

B. We blame ourselves.

As we've already discussed, failure is a very frightening thing. Whenever we fail to gain the acceptance of certain people or fail to perform up to a certain standard, we immediately look for others to blame. But sometimes, even our frantic search for a scapegoat fails, leaving us with no one to blame but ourselves. The act of self-condemnation may be the most severe form of punishment a Christian ever inflicts on himself.

Think back to times when you blamed yourself for mistakes or failures. How did it make you feel?

_____

_____

_____

_____

List several ways in which you punished yourself for these failures.

_____

_____

_____

All of us make mistakes. All of us experience failure. But, this does not mean that we are failures. We sometimes let failure immobilize us by believing that it robs us of our self-esteem. God does not want us as Christians to berate or condemn ourselves. Instead, He expects us to view failure as an opportunity to learn and grow. As we'll see in Part II of this chapter, God has already protected our self-esteem from the ravages of blame and failure.

C. We see God as cruel and punishing.

As we have already learned, the Blame Game Trap promotes the lie that says:

"Those who fail are unworthy of love and deserve to be punished."

By believing this lie, we hurt our relationship with God! As we have just discussed, we all frequently fail. Because we blame others for their failures, we also believe that God must blame us for ours. Therefore, we are convinced that He sees us as unworthy of His love and deserving of punishment. This attitude often leads us to believe that every painful circumstance in our lives is a form of punishment from God. This causes most of us to get angry. We blame God for our failures. We rationalize that He must be expecting too much from us. Because we see God's expectation as too high and His punishment as too severe, we grow convinced that He is cruel and unfair.

Fortunately, God looks at our failures in a totally different way. He loves and accepts us in spite of them.

In Psalms 103, the Bible teaches that God understands our weaknesses and that He continues to love us anyway.

PSALMS 103:13-14 (TLB)
13) He is like a father to us, tender and sympathetic to those who reverence Him.
14) For He knows we are but dust.

Obviously, our self-esteem will be in real trouble if we continually feel unworthy of God's love and are always in fear of His punishment.

THE BLAME GAME TRAP | 5

THE FEAR OF PUNISHMENT TEST

The fear of punishment is the result of the false belief that says, "Those who fail are unworthy of love and deserve to be punished." How affected are you by this belief? In order to get some idea, take the fear of punishment test that follows. But remember, in order for this to help you, you must be honest with yourself on each question.

Instructions

There are seven possible answers to each of the following statements. Read each statement, then choose the answer that is most true about you. Each answer has a number code beside it. Write the correct number code in the blank space provided next to each statement.

(1) Always   (4) Sometimes   (6) Very Seldom

(2) Very Often   (5) Seldom   (7) Never

(3) Often

NUMBER CODE

1. I am afraid of what God may do to punish me. _____

2. After I fail, I worry about God becoming angry with me. _____

3. When I see someone in a difficult situation, I wonder what they did to deserve their problems. _____

4. When something goes wrong, I have a tendency to think God must be punishing me. _____

5. I am very hard on myself when I fail. _____

6. I find myself wanting to blame other people when they fail. _____

7. I get angry at God when someone immoral or dishonest seems to get everything he wants and never gets punished. _____

8. I can't keep myself from criticizing others when I see them doing something wrong. _____

9. Instead of complimenting others on their strengths and accomplishments, I tend to focus on their mistakes and failures. _____

10. God seems cruel and punishing to me. _____

TOTAL (Add up the numbers you have placed in the blanks.) _____

Interpretation of Score

57 - 70 — This score indicates that you are virtually free from the fear of punishment.

47 - 56 — This score indicates that you have a very small fear of punishment. It may be that you feel this fear only in certain situations.

37 - 46 — This score indicates that you have a moderate to strong fear of punishment. It is likely that a good number of your decisions are designed to keep you as far from punishment as possible.

27 - 36 — This score indicates that you have a high fear of punishment. Your emotional lows will almost always be a result of your fear of punishment, or the belief that you are already being punished in some way. Nearly all your decisions are designed to shift blame and punishment away from you.

0 - 26 — This score indicates that you have an overwhelming fear of punishment. Experiences of punishment fill your memories. You may be very depressed.

If you received a score that was lower than you'd like, don't panic. Nearly everyone has struggled with the fear of punishment. However, God does not want us to remain hurting and confused victims of the Blame Game Trap. The rest of this chapter will guide you to freedom from this needless trap through God's great solution.

II. God's solution to the Blame Game Trap — Propitiation

What is God's solution to the subtle, but cruel, Blame Game Trap? What is God's plan to keep us from blaming others, ourselves, and God Himself? God's solution is His loving act of propitiation.

A. What is Propitiation?

Propitiation is another of the Bible's complex words. But it actually has a simple definition. It means to satisfy the wrath of someone who has been unjustly wronged. Propitiation is an act that soothes hostility and satisfies the need for vengeance. Providing His only Son Jesus as the propitiation for our sins was the greatest possible demonstration of God's love for us.

I JOHN 4:9-10 (NASV)

(9) By this the love of God was manifested in us, that God has sent His only begotten Son into the world so that we might live through Him.

(10) In this is love, not that we loved God, but that He loved us and sent His Son to be the propitiation for our sins.

According to I John 4:10, what is the evidence that God loves us?

_____

_____

Why did Jesus have to be the propitiation (wrath satisfier) for our sins?

_____

_____

Jesus was the only choice for our propitiation.

Our sin deserves the full fury of God's anger and punishment. He is the all-powerful, holy, and completely perfect judge of the universe. Therefore, He can never overlook or compromise with sin. For Him to do this would completely ruin His holiness. It would be like smearing black tar on a white satin wedding gown. Our sin is actually a direct attack on God's character. It must be punished. However, God is also full of love and compassion for us. He knew that receiving the punishment we deserved would destroy us all. Therefore, in the most awesome and painful act of love in history, He chose His only Son, Jesus, to endure the horrible anger and agonizing punishment that God's holiness demanded as payment (propitiation) for our sin. Only Jesus, the perfect God-man, could satisfy (propitiate) the total penalty that the combined sin of all mankind had earned.

God's need to vent His righteous anger and punish our sin was satisfied when Christ died on the Cross. And when Jesus returned to life, it was to teach us that as Christians, God now unconditionally loves, accepts and approves of us forever.

B. How does Jesus' love keep us from blaming and punishing others?

Realizing that God no longer blames us for sin and failure but treats us with incredible love, should motivate us to do the same with others. We should be moved to stop blaming them for their failures, and start treating them with God's forgiving love. Let's take another look at I John 4:9-10, and this time add verse 11.

> I JOHN 4:9-11 (NASV)
>
> 9) *By this the love of God was manifested in us, that God has sent His only begotten Son into the world so that we might live through Him.*
>
> 10) *In this is love, not that we loved God, but that He loved us and sent His Son to be the propitiation for our sins.*
>
> 11) *BELOVED, IF GOD SO LOVED US, WE ALSO OUGHT TO LOVE ONE ANOTHER. (author's capitalization)*

According to verse 11, how should we respond to others now that Christ has revealed His love for us through His propitiation?

_____

_____

_____

When we see a Christian who has failed, we need to agree with God's truth about him: <u>He is deeply loved by God, completely forgiven, fully pleasing, totally accepted and complete in Christ</u>. This does not mean that we should become blind to his faults and failures. It does mean that we can change our attitude from one of blame and punishment to one of love and a desire to help. As our self-worth becomes less dependent on other people, their sins and mistakes will become less of a threat to us. Loving and serving others is a natural overflow of a healthy self-esteem. This is so true that God wants us to treat even the most difficult people (including non-Christians), with the same kind of love.

In the Book of Luke, the Bible says:

> LUKE 6:27-28 (NASV)
> 27) *But I say to you who hear, love your enemies, do good to those who hate you,*
> 28) *bless those who curse you, pray for those who mistreat you.*

When we are tempted to blame and punish someone, no matter how cruelly they have hurt us, we need to remind ourselves of this truth — <u>There is nothing anyone can ever do to me that is worse than my sin of rebellion against God, for which I have been completely forgiven.</u>

C. How does Jesus' propitiation keep us from blaming and punishing ourselves?

Self-condemnation, because of our own failures, can be at the very core of our deepest emotional problems. Yet, it is clear that God no longer blames us for our sin. He totally accepts us in love. The Bible clearly states that because of what Jesus did on the cross, God refuses to condemn us any more.

> ROMANS 8:1 (NASV)
> *There is therefore now no condemnation for those who are in Christ Jesus.*

What do you think the words "no condemnation" mean?

_____

_____

_____

"No condemnation" means that God does not condemn us for even one of our sins and failures, either now or in the future, no matter how awful they may be. They were completely forgiven and totally forgotten at the cross.

Throughout the Bible, God tells us again and again that we are deeply loved, completely forgiven, fully pleasing, totally accepted, and complete in Christ. Since God looks at us this way, we should stop condemning ourselves.

All of us fail, but that doesn't mean we are failures. If we choose to learn from our mistakes, they can be big steps toward our maturity.

Failure helps us to realize that our self-esteem does not come from blaming and punishing anyone, especially ourselves. Instead, it's a chance to learn again that healthy self-esteem is given to us joyfully with God's unconditional love and acceptance.

D. How does Jesus' propitiation help us in our relationship with God?

As we have seen, we have believed Satan's lie, which says:

> *"Those who fail are unworthy of love and deserve to be punished."*

Because our failures are frequent, we mistakenly assume that God believes we are unworthy of love and deserve to be punished. But because of Jesus' propitiation we can know that we are not condemned by God. In fact, we know that we should never be afraid of Him because His love for us is perfect. The Bible is clear about this in I John 4.

I JOHN 4:18 (TLB)
We have no fear of someone who loves us perfectly; His perfect love for us eliminates all dread of what He might do to us. If we are afraid, it is for fear of what He might do to us, and shows that we are not fully convinced that He really loves us.

IN CONCLUSION

The Blame Game Trap is a cruel and malicious lie. It says that those who fail are unworthy of love and deserve to be punished. Yet God, in His truth about propitiation can set us free from blaming others, ourselves, or God Himself. As we learn to accept God's love and forgiveness and turn from blaming others, our self-esteem will become more and more like what God intended it to be.

GOD'S UNCONDITIONAL LOVE PROJECT

How do we free ourselves from Satan's lie: *"Those who fail are unworthy of love and deserve to be punished"*? We are freed by understanding and applying God's truth about propitiation. One of the ways to do this is to memorize and think deeply about this paraphrase of Scripture that declares God's great love for us.

I Corinthians 13 describes God's unconditional love for us. To personalize it, replace the word *"love"* with *"My Father."* Memorize it and review it at least once a day for two weeks.

- *My Father is very patient and kind.*
- *My Father is not envious, never boastful.*
- *My Father is not arrogant.*
- *My Father is never rude, nor is my Father self-seeking.*
- *My Father is not quick to take offense.*
- *He keeps no score of wrongs.*
- *My Father does not gloat over my sins, but is always glad when truth prevails.*
- *My Father knows no limit to His endurance, no end to His trust.*
- *My Father is always hopeful and patient.*

As you memorize this ask God to show you if your understanding of Him is wrong in any way. This will enable you to have a better relationship with God and will help to free you from the fear of punishment and the desire to punish others.

6 The Shame Trap...

As we have seen in the last three chapters, Satan has attempted to lure us into several destructive traps. Each trap is built out of widely believed lies. The purpose of these lies is to send us searching for self-esteem in all the wrong places. The three traps are:

1. THE PERFORMANCE TRAP

Its lie is — I must meet certain standards in order to feel good about myself.

2. THE APPROVAL TRAP

Its lie is — I must be accepted by certain others in order to feel good about myself.

3. THE BLAME GAME TRAP

Its lie is — Those who fail are unworthy of love and deserve to be punished.

Most of us have fallen into one or more of these traps because we have believed these lies. Unfortunately, each of these lies leads us into a new trap that may be more dangerous and painful than any of the others. It is called the Shame Trap.

IN THIS CHAPTER, WE'LL DISCUSS THE DAMAGING POWER OF THE SHAME TRAP, AND GOD'S SOLUTION FOR RESCUING US FROM ITS CRIPPLING EFFECTS.

6 THE SHAME TRAP

I. What is the Shame Trap?

The Shame Trap is the wrong belief that there is something wrong with us that can never be repaired. When we fall into the Shame Trap it is because we have believed another of Satan's destructive lies. That lie is:

> *"I must always be what I have been and live with whatever self-worth I have. I am what I am. I cannot change. I am hopeless."*

To understand the Shame Trap, we must understand what we mean by the word shame in this chapter. Shame is the deep feeling of guilt, sadness, and hopelessness that we experience when we become convinced that past failures, bad habits or poor appearance have made a permanent scar on our self-worth.

Examples of being caught in the Shame Trap.

Here are several examples of how shame causes students to believe that there is something permanently wrong with them:

- *Since I have lost my virginity, I will never be worthy of someone who will really love me.*
- *Ever since I was held back one year, I have been unable to do well in school.*
- *I'd have a lot more friends if I were better looking.*
- *I'll never be a very good athlete, but I'd be a lot more popular if I was.*
- *My dad said I was a failure and he is right. I will never succeed at anything.*
- *I do drugs, and I know it's ruining my life, but I can't change.*
- *When my parents got divorced, I realized what a loser I really was.*

Because this kind of shame can be tremendously destructive, let's examine what causes it.

6 THE SHAME TRAP

A. Three reasons we experience shame.

1. We experience shame when we believe we have failed too often in the past.

All of us have painful memories of past situations that didn't seem to work out. In one way or another, we felt disappointed. While some of these situations were the result of our own sin or mistakes, many of them were out of our control. But as time passes, we tend to remember most of these disappointments as personal failures. The more we believe we've failed in the past, the more we seem to expect to fail in the future. This can cause us to experience a deep sense of guilt and hopelessness. In other words — we feel ashamed.

Obviously, feeling ashamed of ourselves is very painful and can cause serious damage to our self-worth. Because the emotional pain from past failures is so severe, we try to cope with our shame by expecting far too little from ourselves. Our decisions are increasingly based on one condition — "How can I avoid the failure and rejection that cause me so much shame?"

Here are several examples of how shame can cause us to make bad decisions:

- *Sally decided to cancel this year's Fourth of July picnic because it rained on the 4th last year.*

- *The football coach decided not to play any of the teams that beat his squad last year because he thought they would lose again and thereby embarrass him.*

- *After Karen refused a date with Jim, he decided that he would quit dating altogether.*

- *When Bill discovered he had failed his first science test, he felt really dumb and started skipping class.*

What would you say is wrong with the way each of these decisions were made?

_____

_____

In each of these examples, these people lowered their expectations because of a past failure. Unfortunately, having lower expectations never works. It only proves that we are caught in the Shame Trap, and that we still believe Satan's lie: *"I am what I am. I cannot change. I am hopeless."*

2. We experience shame when we feel we are unable to break the destructive bad habits that are ruining our lives.

Most of us have a few bad habits that we would like to change. But sometimes a certain bad habit may seem to enslave us. We feel helpless to break it even though it is clearly hurting us, our relationship with God, and those around us. The longer we feel trapped by any destructive bad habit, the more likely we are to give in to it. Unfortunately, the more we give in, the more our self-esteem drops. The more our self-esteem drops, the more likely we are to remain enslaved by our bad habits. We feel guilty, sad, and hopeless. In other words, we feel ashamed.

THE SHAME TRAP

Do you have a bad habit that you've had trouble getting rid of? Write it down and explain why you think it's been so difficult to break!

_____

_____

_____

_____

Some of us have gotten involved with bad habits in order to escape from the pain of past failures. We may spend all our time playing video games, drinking alcohol, doing drugs, becoming involved in pornography, etc., to cover up this pain. However, while our bad habits may dull the pain for awhile, we often wind up as ashamed of them as we are of our past failures. This not only leads to more pain, but leaves us in a vicious and hopeless circle of despair.

Describe some bad habits that people get involved with in order to help feel better about themselves.

_____

_____

_____

Why do you think these bad habits will in the end lead them into shame and lower self-esteem?

_____

_____

_____

In the book of Proverbs, King Solomon wrote about the kind of decision we make when we choose to start a bad habit.

> PROVERBS 16:25 (TLB)
> *Before every man there lies a wide and pleasant road he thinks is right, but it ends in death.*

All of us have taken the wide and pleasant road of bad habits. Why do you think Solomon says this road ends in death?

_____

_____

_____

Any activity that displeases God is destructive. Bad habits cause us to believe Satan's lies about our self-esteem. He wants us to have bad habits in hopes that we will become more and more defeated and hopeless. They only lead us further into the Shame Trap.

3. We experience shame when we believe that the way we look has held us back from success.

In our society, our appearance is considered very important. Magazine ads, billboards, television commercials and programs are filled with people who we would call very attractive. Our problems begin when we compare ourselves to these unrealistic *"beautiful people"* standards. We wrongly believe that to be successful and accepted, we must be as attractive as these men and women. Unfortunately, very few of us are. Most of us tend to feel ashamed of some aspect of our appearance.

List some things about your appearance you would change if you could.

_____

_____

_____

_____

THE SHAME TRAP

THE I-AM-ASHAMED TEST

Much of our shame is the result of the false belief that says, "I must always be what I have been and live with whatever self-worth I have. I am what I am. I cannot change. I am hopeless." How affected are you by this belief? In order to get some idea, take the shame test that follows. But remember, in order for this to help you, you must be honest with yourself on each question.

Instructions

There are seven possible answers to each of the following statements. Read each statement, then choose the answer that is most true about you. Each answer has a number code beside it. Write the correct number code in the blank space provided next to each statement.

(1) Always	(4) Sometimes	(6) Very Seldom
(2) Very Often	(5) Seldom	(7) Never
(3) Often		

NUMBER CODE

1. I think about past failures or experiences of rejection. _____

2. I have certain memories about my past which cause me to feel strong painful emotions (guilt, shame, anger, fear, etc.). _____

3. I seem to make the same mistakes. _____

4. I have certain attitudes and behaviors that I want to change, but I don't think I can. _____

5. I feel inferior. _____

6. I don't like some things about the way I look. _____

7. I am generally disgusted with myself. _____

8. I feel certain experiences have basically ruined my life. _____

9. I think I am an immoral person. _____

10. I feel I have lost the opportunity to experience a complete and wonderful life. _____

TOTAL (Add up the numbers you have placed in the blanks.)

Interpretation of Score

57 - 70 — This score indicates that you are virtually free from feelings of shame.

47 - 56 — This score indicates that you rarely experience shame. It may be that shame controls you only in certain situations.

37 - 46 — This score indicates that shame may be causing many of your emotional upsets. It is likely that a good number of your decisions have been influenced by shame.

27 - 36 — This score indicates that you feel a lot of shame. Your emotional lows will almost always be a result of your feeling ashamed of yourself. Nearly all your decisions are influenced by your deep feelings of shame.

0 - 26 — This score indicates that your feelings of shame are overwhelming. Experiences of shame fill your memories. You may be depressed.

If you received a score that was lower than you'd like, don't panic. Nearly everyone has struggled with the painful feelings of shame. However, God does not want us to remain as hurting and confused victims of the Shame Trap. The rest of this chapter will guide you through God's great solution for freeing you from this tragic trap.

II. God's Solution to the Shame Trap — Regeneration

As we have seen, there are at least three major areas where we are most vulnerable to the Shame Trap:

- *Past failures, both real and imagined.*
- *Bad habits.*
- *Poor appearance and the belief that there is something wrong with the way we look.*

However, God has made it possible for us to escape from the Shame Trap through what the Bible calls **Regeneration**.

WHAT IS REGENERATION?

Regeneration is a special work of God that literally makes each believer a new person the instant he trusts Christ to be his Savior. The Bible talks about this new person in II Corinthians 5.

II CORINTHIANS 5:17 (NASV)
Therefore if any man is in Christ, he is a new creature; the old things passed away; behold, new things have come.

How does the Bible describe a person who has put his faith in Christ?

_____

_____

_____

In that verse, the Bible says "the old things passed away." What do you think *"old things"* is referring to?

_____

_____

What do you think *"new things have come"* means?

_____

_____

_____

Regeneration is not a self-improvement program or a clean-up campaign for our sinful thoughts and habits. It is not a matter of trying to patch up our old lives with all its problems. Instead, regeneration is the beginning of a completely new life in Christ.

THE STORY OF ZACCHAEUS

One of the best examples of regeneration is the Bible's story of a man named Zacchaeus, found in Luke 19.

LUKE 19:1-9 (TLB)

1, 2) As Jesus was passing through Jericho, a man named Zacchaeus, one of the most influential Jews in the Roman tax-collecting business (and, of course, a very rich man),

3) tried to get a look at Jesus, but he was too short to see over the crowds.

4) So he ran ahead and climbed into a sycamore tree beside the road, to watch from there.

5) When Jesus came by he looked up at Zacchaeus and called him by name! "Zacchaeus!" he said. "Quick! Come down! For I am going to be a guest in your home today!"

6) Zacchaeus hurriedly climbed down and took Jesus to his house in great excitement and joy.

7) But the crowds were displeased. "He has gone to be the guest of a notorious sinner," they grumbled.

8) Meanwhile, Zacchaeus stood before the Lord and said, "Sir, from now on I will give half my wealth to the poor, and if I find I have overcharged anyone on his taxes, I will penalize myself by giving him back four times as much!"

9) Jesus told him, "This shows that salvation has come to this house today."

The town's people hated Zacchaeus because he had grown rich by cheating them on their taxes. But the day he met Christ and accepted Him as Saviour, Zacchaeus began to act like a completely new person. He paid back four times as much money as he had stolen, and gave away half of his entire fortune to charity.

Zacchaeus was regenerated and became a radically new person. He started a whole new life empowered by God. Like Zacchaeus, regeneration can make us new people, with new values, new goals, and new behavior.

A. Regeneration helps us put past failures into perspective.

Regeneration means that in God's eyes, what we were and what we did in the past are gone forever. Of course, it's important to learn from our past mistakes, but our new self has been especially designed to focus on the future that God has planned for us.

The Apostle Paul tells about this radical change from past failure to future hopes in Titus chapter 3.

TITUS 3:3-5 & 7 (NASV)

3) *For we also once were foolish ourselves, disobedient, deceived, enslaved to various lusts and pleasures, spending our life in malice and envy, hateful, hating one another.*

4) *But when the kindness of God our Savior and His love for mankind appeared,*

5) *He saved us, not on the basis of deeds which we have done in righteousness, but according to His mercy, by the washing of regeneration and renewing by the Holy Spirit,*

7) *that being justified by His grace, we might be made heirs according to the hope of eternal life.*

According to verse 3, what were we like before we came to Christ?

_____

_____

_____

Once God has made us into new people through regeneration, what do we have to look forward to according to Titus 3:7?

_____

_____

_____

We need to understand that our regeneration in Christ is complete and perfect. God has made us new. From His perspective we do not change and cannot be improved upon. His total acceptance of us is based on our new regenerated life in Christ. When we begin to believe these truths, our self-worth will improve dramatically.

B. Regeneration helps us overcome bad habits.

Through regeneration, we are God's new people. Because we are His new people, He wants us to see ourselves in a completely new way. Because He has made us new creatures and has given us new power to do His will, we don't have to see ourselves as mistake-prone failures. We are not losers in life. God wants us to understand clearly that through Christ we are winners for eternity. Philippians 1:6 tells us why this is true:

PHILIPPIANS 1:6 (TLB)

And I am sure that God who began the good work within you will keep right on helping you grow in His grace until His task within you is finally finished on that day when Jesus Christ returns.

Because we are regenerated (new people in Christ), God wants us to know that we don't have to give in to destructive bad habits. Since God sees us as winners, the Bible tells us that we no longer need to behave like losers who are caught up in destructive bad habits.

EPHESIANS 4:22-24 (NIV)

22) *You were taught, with regard to your former way of life, to put off your old self, which is being corrupted by its deceitful desires;*

23) *to be made new in the attitude of your minds;*

24) *and to put on the new self, created to be like God in true righteousness and holiness.*

In verse 22, what does it mean to have the old self corrupted by deceitful desires?

_____

_____

_____

Before we were regenerated in Christ, we were helpless against our bad habits. The *"old self"* lacked both God's truth and God's power. Not only were we unable to change, we didn't really want to.

According to verse 23, how does regeneration change us?

_____

_____

_____

According to verse 24, what is one of the things we can do to help us break destructive habits?

_____

_____

_____

Knowing that God has made us new means we can have a new attitude toward everything in our life. Having God's righteousness means we can take new actions to rid ourselves of our destructive bad habits. Through Christ we have the power to make the right decisions. Through these right decisions, we can put our sinful bad habits behind us, and live a shame-free life.

C. Regeneration enables us to view our appearance as a gift from God.

As we have seen, when God made us His new people, our new self came complete with a new set of values. With these values, we can even begin to see our appearance the way God does. The world controlled by Satan puts a very high value on good looks. But God wants us to understand that His values are different. The Bible talks about God's creation of us in Ephesians 2:

EPHESIANS 2:10 (NIV)

For we are God's workmanship, created in Christ Jesus to do good works, which God prepared in advance for us to do.

What does this verse mean when it says *"we are God's workmanship"*?

_____

_____

_____

Our God is perfect. And everything about us, including our appearance, has been created according to God's perfect plan for our life. We will always be able to find people who are *"better"* looking than we are. Therefore, if we try to gain self-esteem from our appearance, we will always be disappointed. But, God wants us to get our self-esteem from believing that He is a perfect creator. He wants us to say to ourselves: *"God has made me just right for His purposes."*

IN CONCLUSION

As we have seen, Satan uses the Shame Trap to convince us that our past failures, our bad habits, or our poor appearance has somehow damaged us. He wants us to believe that we can never be what God wants us to be. But God wants us to know that this is a lie.

Our Regeneration, through Christ, means God has made us brand new people. When He looks at us, our new self is all He sees. God views us as completely forgiven, deeply loved, totally accepted, fully pleasing and complete in Christ. Therefore, if we guard our thoughts by studying and thinking about these truths in the Bible, we can have tremendous and overwhelming self-esteem that is free of shame.

The following are three Bible verses that can be removed from your manual. Each verse represents a correct belief that will help you escape from the Shame Trap. Memorize both the verses and the correct belief beneath them. Then, spend some time thinking about how it applies to your life.

II CORINTHIANS 5:17 (NASV)

Therefore if any man is in Christ, he is a new creature; the old things passed away; behold, new things have come.

<u>Correct Belief</u> — *I thank God that He has made me a completely new person, able to have new values, new goals, and new behavior.*

TITUS 3:3-5 (NASV)

3) *For we also once were foolish ourselves, disobedient, deceived, enslaved to various lusts and pleasures, spending our life in malice and envy, hateful, hating one another.*

4) *But when the kindness of God our Savior and His love for mankind appeared,*

5) *He saved us, not on the basis of deeds which we have done in righteousness, but according to His mercy, by the washing of regeneration and renewing by the Holy Spirit.*

<u>Correct Belief</u> — *I thank God that because of His love for me, I can start loving myself and begin to break my bad habits.*

PHILIPPIANS 1:6 (TLB)

And I am sure that God who began the good work within you will keep right on helping you grow in His grace until His task within you is finally finished on that day when Jesus Christ returns.

<u>Correct Belief</u> — *I thank God that He is working within me each day to help me become more and more like Jesus.*

7 | Learning How to Examine and Change Our Beliefs...

If we believe and act on God's truths about our self-esteem, we can be set free from Satan's destructive traps. Getting rid of our destructive wrong beliefs and replacing them with healthy right beliefs makes it possible for us to love and accept ourselves, others, and God in the way He intended.

The question is, where can we find the power to recognize and resist the clever lies Satan uses to tear down our self-esteem? And how can we implant God's healing truths into our minds each day until they become part of our lifestyle?

IN THIS FINAL DISCUSSION, WE WILL LEARN THAT THROUGH THE HOLY SPIRIT, GOD HAS GIVEN US THE POWER TO CHANGE OUR WRONG BELIEFS. WE ALSO WILL LEARN HOW TO PRACTICALLY APPLY GOD'S TRUTH ABOUT OUR SELF-ESTEEM EVERY DAY.

I. The Holy Spirit is the Source for Change.

It should be obvious to us that real change in our behavior and lifestyle is not easy to do. It is true that through discipline and determination we may be able to change some of our outward habits. But our deeply held beliefs about our self-esteem can only be changed through a special relationship with Christ. The Bible talks about this very special relationship in John 15:5.

JOHN 15:5 (TLB)

Yes, I am the Vine; you are the branches. Whoever lives in me and I in Him shall produce a large crop of fruit. For apart from me you can't do a thing.

According to this verse, how much can we do apart from Christ?

_____

_____

_____

LEARNING HOW TO EXAMINE AND CHANGE OUR BELIEFS

Since the Bible is very clear that without Christ we can't change, what does Christ do to bring this change about? In John 14:16, Jesus told His disciples about a very special helper He was going to send to all Christians.

JOHN 14:16 (NASV)

And I will ask the Father, and He will give you another Helper, that He may be with you forever.

That helper referred to in this verse is the Holy Spirit. Who is the Holy Spirit and how can He use His power to help us change?

A. Who is the Holy Spirit?

In I Corinthians 2:10-11, the Bible explains to us that the Holy Spirit knows all of God's thoughts.

I CORINTHIANS 2:10-11 (TLB)

10) *But we know about these things because God has sent His Spirit to tell us, and His Spirit searches out and shows us all of God's deepest secrets.*

11) *No one can really know what anyone else is thinking, or what he is really like, except that person himself. And no one can know God's thoughts except God's own Spirit.*

What do you think this verse means when it says that the *"Spirit searches out and shows us all of God's deepest secrets"*?

_____

_____

_____

The Holy Spirit knows and understands everything about God. There is nothing about God that is hidden from Him. The only way that this could be possible is if the Holy Spirit is God Himself.

If the Holy Spirit knows and understands everything about God, and is actually God Himself, how much do you think He knows about us?

_____

_____

Since the Holy Spirit is God and knows everything about us, He not only wants to help us, but He is able to give us the power to change.

B. How does the Holy Spirit give us the power to change our wrong beliefs into right ones?

The Holy Spirit is eager for us to give Him control of our lives so He can help us make improvements in our lives.

The Bible talks about these improvements in Galatians 5.

> GALATIANS 5:22-23 (TLB)
>
> *But when the Holy Spirit controls our lives He will produce this kind of fruit in us: love, joy, peace, patience, kindness, goodness, faithfulness, gentleness and self-control.*

As we have discussed throughout this book, we all have certain beliefs that affect our self-esteem. Some of these beliefs are true, but some of them are dangerously false. The Holy Spirit is deeply concerned with helping us expose our false beliefs and replace them with truth. The Bible states this very clearly in John 16:13.

JOHN 16:13 (TLB)

When the Holy Spirit, who is truth, comes, He shall guide you into all truth . . .

How much truth, including truth about our self-worth, will the Holy Spirit guide us into?

The main source of God's truth is the Bible. The Bible is like a powerful searchlight. The Holy Spirit focuses this powerful light upon our beliefs seeking to expose any of Satan's lies that may be hiding there. Then He helps us to replace those lies with God's truth.

C. How do we let the Holy Spirit work in our lives?

When we accept Christ, the Holy Spirit automatically comes to live within us. But the Bible also teaches that He wants to have control of our lives. God wants us to obey His command in Ephesians 5:18.

> EPHESIANS 5:18 (TLB)
>
> *Don't drink too much wine, for many evils lie along that path; be filled instead with the Holy Spirit, and controlled by Him.*

According to this verse, what do you think it means to be filled by the Holy Spirit?

_____

_____

_____

To be filled with the Spirit means to be controlled by Him. It means we are believing and obeying the truth He is teaching us, and that we are allowing Him to give us the power to change our lives.

D. We often stop the Holy Spirit from controlling our lives!

The Holy Spirit wants to lead us into all truth, including truth about our self-esteem. However, we often stop the Holy Spirit from controlling our lives. The Bible clearly tells us this is wrong.

I THESSALONIANS 5:19 (NASV)

Do not quench the Spirit;

What do you think *"quenching the Spirit"* means?

_____

_____

When we quench the Holy Spirit, it means that we stop Him from controlling our lives. This happens when we refuse to deal with our sins which He has revealed to us. We stop Him from giving us the power to change because we turn our back on the truth by refusing to act on it.

But God, in His great love for us wants us to understand that being controlled by the Holy Spirit is only a prayer away. A verse that instructs us on how to properly deal with our sin is found in I John 1:9.

I JOHN 1:9 (TLB)
But if we confess our sins to Him, He can be depended on to forgive us and to cleanse us from every wrong.

What do you think it means to confess our sins?

_____

_____

_____

When we confess our sins, it means that we agree with Christ that what we have done is wrong, that we are sinners, and that He has already paid for those sins at the cross. It also signifies that we are willing to turn away from our rebellion and wrong thinking which hurt Him deeply. In addition, we will do our best to act upon the truth the Holy Spirit is seeking to teach us. Once we confess our sins, the Holy Spirit will control us once more. We won't necessarily feel any different when this happens, but the Holy Spirit will be there, quietly guiding us into the truth and giving us the power to make lasting changes.

II. The Battle for Self-Esteem is Won or Lost in Our Minds.

It is important for us to realize that even though we have been made new in Christ, there is still a battle going on in our minds. The Holy Spirit is living within us. Each day He leads us into more truth, including truth about our self-esteem. Nevertheless, some of Satan's lies continue to hide within our minds and confuse us about our sense of significance. The result is that we still have many wrong beliefs that can wind up as wrong behavior. The Bible confirms this in Proverbs 23:7.

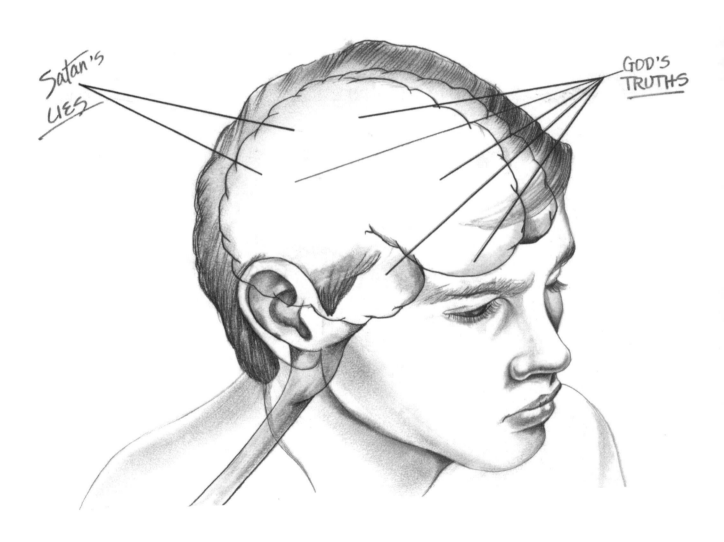

7 LEARNING HOW TO EXAMINE AND CHANGE OUR BELIEFS

> PROVERBS 23:7 (NASV)
> *For as (a man) thinks within himself, so he is.*

By understanding how our minds work to shape our self-esteem, we can become much more successful at identifying our wrong beliefs!

How Does Our Mind Work to Shape Our Self-esteem?

Obviously our minds are very complex. The following diagram will be used to help us more clearly understand how the shaping of our self-esteem takes place.

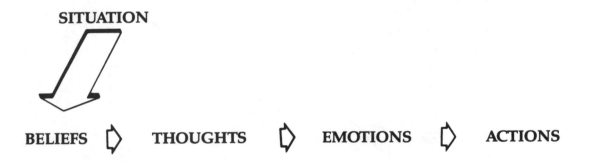

SITUATION

BELIEFS ⟹ THOUGHTS ⟹ EMOTIONS ⟹ ACTIONS

A. What are Situations?

SITUATION

Beliefs ⟶ Thoughts ⟶ Emotions ⟶ Actions

Situations are the real events, circumstances, or experiences that occur everyday in our lives.

We encounter many situations each day. Sometimes these situations involve relationships between people. For example:

- *Jim told Janet that she looks nice today.*
- *Kevin's English teacher told him that he did a good job on his latest project.*

Sometimes situations can be events.

- *Todd locked his keys in the car.*
- *Krista's school bus was half an hour late.*

List three situations that have occurred in your life in the past week.

_____

_____

_____

Regardless of the kind of situation we face, the way we react or respond to it is entirely determined by our beliefs.

B. What are Beliefs?

Situation

BELIEFS ⟶ Thoughts ⟶ Emotions ⟶ Actions

Beliefs are deeply held ideas that we perceive as true, existing both in our conscious and sub-conscious minds.

All of us have deeply held beliefs. And many of these beliefs are true. For example:

- *God is good.*
- *God is perfect.*
- *America is called "The land of opportunity."*

LEARNING HOW TO EXAMINE AND CHANGE OUR BELIEFS

List three beliefs you know are true.

_____

_____

_____

However, some of our deeply held beliefs are not true. They are false beliefs. Some of these false beliefs can be destructive to our self-esteem. The best examples of these false beliefs are the ones which we have been discussing throughout this manual:

1. *I must meet certain standards in order to feel good about myself.*
   (The Performance Trap)

2. *I must be approved by certain others in order to feel good about myself.*
   (The Approval Trap)

3. *Those who fail are unworthy of love and deserve to be punished.*
   (The Blame Game Trap)

4. *I am what I am. I cannot change. I am hopeless.*
   (The Shame Trap)

Sometimes these beliefs are in our conscious mind where we are aware of them. But others are locked away in our sub-conscious mind. We are unaware that they are there. Nevertheless, our beliefs, both conscious and sub-conscious, are what trigger our thoughts.

C. What are Thoughts?

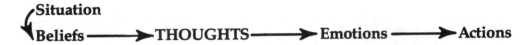

Thoughts are conscious ideas that occur in our minds and are shaped by our beliefs as we interpret life's situations.

As we have just discovered, all our thoughts can be traced back to our beliefs — beliefs based on the truth of Scripture, other truths from life, or the lies of Satan. Understanding that thoughts are the products of beliefs gives us a tool for exposing them.

The following example states a situation and some possible thoughts about this situation.

Situation — *The school bus was 30 minutes late.*

Sample Thoughts

- *The bus driver must be lazy and irresponsible.*
- *I could be late and the teacher will be mad at me.*
- *The bus probably broke down, but in the end everything will be okay.*

All our thoughts are attempts to interpret a given situation. Using our beliefs as a filter, we try to understand what a situation means and how it will affect us. It is our thoughts that trigger our emotions.

D. What are Emotions?

Situation
Beliefs ——→ Thoughts ——→ EMOTIONS ——→ Actions

Emotions are the feelings we have, based on what we believe about a situation.

We generally believe that situations trigger our emotions. But this is not true. It is our beliefs that effect our emotions. Therefore, it we evaluate our emotions, they can help us determine whether our beliefs are true or false. Negative emotions like anger or fear often mean we have some kind of false belief about our self-esteem.

E. What are Actions?

Situation
Beliefs ——→ Thoughts ——→ Emotions ——→ ACTIONS

Actions are the things we do, based on how we feel about a situation. Our emotions are the launching pads for our actions. When we receive a message from our emotions to act, we have three choices:

1. _We can ignore the message._

2. _We can do what our emotions want us to do._

3. _We can do the opposite of what our emotions want us to do._

7 LEARNING HOW TO EXAMINE AND CHANGE OUR BELIEFS

THE DISCOVERING-OUR-FALSE-BELIEFS PROJECT

As we have seen, it is false beliefs that negatively affect our thoughts, emotions, and actions by causing us to misinterpret life's situations.

The following stories illustrate how our false beliefs cause this to happen. Read each story and think about how certain false beliefs caused the problems.

THE FOUR FALSE BELIEFS ARE:

1. *I must meet certain standards in order to feel good about myself.* **(The Performance Trap)**

2. *I must be approved by certain others in order to feel good about myself.* **(The Approval Trap)**

3. *Those who fail are unworthy of love and deserve to be punished.* **(The Blame Game Trap)**

4. *I am what I am. I cannot change. I am hopeless.* **(The Shame Trap)**

Bill's Problem

Bill's Situation: Bill was a first chair trumpet player in his high school band. The band was having an important practice on Saturday. The band teacher made it clear that there would be no excuses for missing. Bill arranged to get a ride with his friend Tom. When Saturday came, Tom didn't show up. Bill finally called and found out that Tom had overslept. By the time Tom arrived at Bill's house, it was too late for them to make it to band practice.

Bill's Thoughts:

- "If Tom were really a friend, he wouldn't be this irresponsible."

- "I'll probably be moved down to second or third chair for missing practice. I couldn't stand that."

- "I hope the teacher doesn't take too many points off my grade. I wanted to have the highest grade in class."

- "Because of Tom, I'm going to get a poor grade."

- "I don't know if Tom and I can ever be friends again."

Bill's Emotions:

- *"Missing this practice makes me feel angry at Tom for being so irresponsible."*
- *"I feel stupid for not planning another way to get to band practice."*
- *"I feel like a failure in band."*

Bill's Actions:

- *He talks to his counselor about dropping band.*
- *He stops practicing his trumpet.*
- *He avoids his band teacher.*
- *He avoids Tom and tells his other friends how Tom failed him.*

Bill's False Beliefs:

Which two of the four false beliefs were causing Bill to think wrong thoughts, feel wrong emotions, and take wrong actions?

1. *"I must meet certain standards in order to feel good about myself"*
   (The Performance Trap)
2. *"Those who fail are unworthy of love and deserve to be punished"*
   (The Blame Game Trap)

Karen's Problem

Karen's Situation: Karen had a small group of good friends. However, when Karen made the cheerleading squad, she became very busy. Cheerleading practice and the games themselves gave her much less time to spend with her friends. Unfortunately, Karen's good friends thought she was just acting stuck-up. Later, Karen found out that her good friends were having a party and she was not invited.

Karen's Thoughts:

- *"My friends act like they don't care about me anymore."*
- *"I've let my closest friends down."*
- *"I'll never have good friends again."*
- *"Joining the cheerleading team was a mistake."*
- *"Why do I always make the wrong choices in my life?"*

Karen's Emotions:

- *"I feel lonely."*
- *"I feel rejected and worthless."*
- *"I feel stupid for ever trying out for cheerleading."*
- *"I feel like I'll never do anything right."*

Karen's Actions:

- *She walks the other way when she sees her old friends.*
- *She withdraws and seldom talks to anyone.*
- *She begins to miss cheerleading practice and does a poor job of cheering at the games.*

Karen's False Beliefs:

Which two of the four false beliefs were causing Karen to think wrong thoughts, feel wrong emotions, and take wrong actions?

1. *"I must be approved by certain others in order to feel good about myself."*
   (The Approval Trap)

2. *"I am what I am. I cannot change. I am hopeless."*
   (The Shame Trap)

LEARNING HOW TO EXAMINE AND CHANGE OUR BELIEFS

These are two basic illustrations of how our false beliefs can affect our thoughts, emotions, and actions. In the project that follows, write in a situation, possibly from your own life, along with thoughts, emotions, and actions. Then see if you can figure out which of the four false beliefs apply to this situation.

Your Situation:

_____

_____

Your Thoughts:

_____

_____

Your Emotions:

_____

_____

Your Actions:

_____

_____

Which of the four false beliefs did you believe in this situation?

_____

_____

III. We Can Learn to Replace False Beliefs with God's Truth about Our Self-Esteem.

As we've already seen, the battle for self-esteem is primarily a battle between our wrong and right beliefs. Most of this battle takes place in our minds and has a tremendous impact on our thoughts, emotions, and actions. The Bible says that in order to win this battle, we must capture those wrong beliefs in our minds and replace them with right beliefs.

> **II CORINTHIANS 10:5 (NIV)**
>
> *We demolish arguments and every pretension that sets itself up against the knowledge of God, and we take captive every thought to make it obedient to Christ.*

What do you think it means to *"take every thought captive to make it obedient to Christ"*?

_____

_____

_____

Taking our thoughts captive means that we must find and examine our beliefs. We must make sure that these beliefs are actually true. Making our thoughts obedient to Christ means that we must throw out our wrong beliefs and replace them with God's truth. The Bible gives us good instruction about how we should replace our false beliefs.

> **PHILIPPIANS 4:8 (TLB)**
>
> *...Fix your thoughts on what is true and good and right. Think about things that are pure and lovely, and dwell on the fine, good things in others. Think about all you can praise God for and be glad about.*

What do you think it means to *"fix our thoughts"*?

_____

_____

Very simply, fixing our thoughts means that God wants us to concentrate our thinking on His truth. Most of our wrong beliefs have been in our minds for some time. Therefore, it can be difficult to find and remove them from our thinking. However, each day will present us with new situations that can help us recognize our wrong beliefs and replace them with God's truth.

How Do We Replace False Beliefs With God's Truth About Our Self-esteem?

As we have previously discussed, recognizing and evaluating our emotions can help us discover our false beliefs. Negative emotions are especially good indications that we are basing our self-esteem on Satan's lies, rather than God's truth. The following diagram helps to explain how evaluating our emotions can help us discover our false beliefs. We must discover these before we can replace them with God's freeing truth.

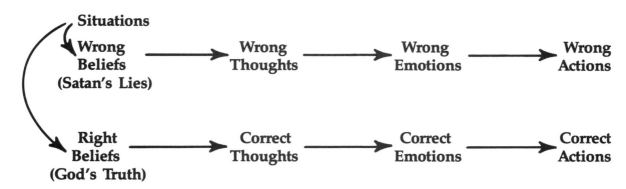

7 LEARNING HOW TO EXAMINE AND CHANGE OUR BELIEFS

As you can see, when we have a wrong belief it causes wrong thinking, wrong emotions, and wrong actions. But by evaluating our wrong emotions, we can often correct our beliefs. Correct beliefs will almost always produce correct thoughts, emotions, and actions.

However, it is important to realize that even negative emotions may not be bad in and of themselves. Almost any emotion can be appropriate if the situation is appropriate. For example, if someone close to you dies, deep sorrow and grief are understandable. If a drunk driver kills a small child, anger is certainly understandable. The important thing to remember is that all emotions must be traced back to our beliefs to determine if they are God's truth or Satan's lies.

THE REPLACING-OUR-FALSE-BELIEFS PROJECT

The following stories are the same ones used in the DISCOVERING-OUR-FALSE-BELIEFS project earlier in this chapter. Re-read these stories. Then write in Bill and Karen's wrong emotions and wrong beliefs in the space provided. Next, review the four correct beliefs listed below. Decide which of these correct beliefs Bill and Karen need in order to replace their wrong beliefs.

THE FOUR CORRECT BELIEFS ARE:

1. *I am completely forgiven and fully pleasing to God.* **(Justification)**

2. *I am totally accepted by God.* **(Reconciliation)**

3. *I am deeply loved by God.* **(Propitiation)**

4. *I am a new, absolutely complete person in Christ.* **(Regeneration)**

Bill's Problem

Bill's Situation: Bill was a first chair trumpet player in his high school band. The band was having an important practice on Saturday. The band teacher made it clear that there would be no excuses for missing. Bill arranged to get a ride with his friend Tom. When Saturday came, Tom didn't show up. Bill finally called and found out that Tom had overslept. By the time Tom arrived at Bill's house, it was too late for them to make it to band practice.

What were Bill's wrong emotions? (See page 137)

1. _____

2. _____

3. _____

What were Bill's wrong beliefs? (See page 137)

1. _____

2. _____

3. _____

Which of the four correct beliefs **(God's truths)** does Bill need to replace his wrong beliefs?

1. _____

2. _____

By replacing his wrong beliefs with the right beliefs, Bill's throughts, emotions, and actions should improve for the better. He will begin to be positive toward Tom and have an improved sense of self-esteem.

Karen's Problem

Karen's Situation: Karen had a small group of good friends. However, when Karen made the cheerleading squad, she became very busy. Cheerleading practice and the games themselves gave her much less time to spend with her friends. Unfortunately, Karen's good friends thought she was just acting stuck-up. Later, Karen found out that her good friends were having a party and she was not invited.

What were Karen's emotions? (See page 138)

1. _____

2. _____

3. _____

4. _____

What were Karen's wrong beliefs? (See page 138)

1. _____

2. _____

Which of the four correct beliefs **(God's truths)** does Karen need to replace her wrong beliefs?

1. _____

2. _____

By replacing her wrong beliefs with right beliefs, Karen's thoughts, emotions and actions should change for the better. Her sense of self-esteem will steadily improve.

IN CONCLUSION

As we have seen, almost all of us have believed some of Satan's lies about our self-worth. These false beliefs have caused us to react to many of life's situations in the wrong way. Therefore, most of us are plagued with a loss of significance and low self-esteem. But God deeply wants us to understand that it is possible to reject our wrong beliefs and replace them with God's healing and freeing truth.

However, we must never forget that rejecting our wrong beliefs and replacing them with God's beliefs is a battle! It is spiritual warfare, and Satan will try to confuse us every step of the way. Therefore, we must rely on the power of the Holy Spirit to help us each day. If we are willing to think deeply on God's Word and replace our false beliefs with His truth, we will find our self-esteem becoming stronger and healthier than we ever believed possible. We must never forget that Christ has already done the hard part. Because of His work on the cross, we are deeply loved by God, completely forgiven, fully pleasing, totally accepted, and complete in Christ.

LEARNING HOW TO EXAMINE AND CHANGE OUR BELIEFS

ABOUT RAPHA

Rapha provides a safe and secure environment, in both hospital and outpatient settings, for individuals needing extensive care. This care is provided by caring profesionals who are committed to a uniquely Christ-centered approach to therapy.

Rapha provides an adolescent and adult psychiatric and substance abuse program that clearly defines and educates the patient about the emotional, physical and spiritual effects of chemical dependency.

Rapha confronts strongly the 'security' and 'significance' issues brought about by peer and parental pressures, and defines clearly the need to understand 'self-worth' from a perspective of Christian personhood rather than the performance demands of a world system.

Rapha has counselors, therapists and support staff that meet all requirements of state and federal government agencies and are properly credentialized to administer the carefully controlled treatment programs provided for adolescents and adults.

Rapha adult and adolescent programs are covered by most insurance companies.

Rapha has locations across the U.S. where treatment is immediately available.

FOR ADDITIONAL INFORMATION ABOUT RAPHA. . . CALL TOLL FREE:
U.S. — 1-800-227-2657
OR WRITE:
P.O. BOX 580355 — HOUSTON, TX 77258

ABOUT SHEPHERD MINISTRIES

Shepherd Ministries is an organization meeting the needs of youth and serving as a resource to church youth groups through several different areas:

- **Publications** — With the writing skill of Dawson McAllister and others, Shepherd offers youth resource manuals for spiritual growth and maturity. Currently fifteen books are published to assist youth in their relationships with God, parents, and others. Leaders' guides are available for many of these topics. Beyond the written page, Shepherd produces videos which touch the the pulse of the American student. Whether the topic concerns one's self-esteem, how to get along with parents, or any other of the thirteen topics, the videos capture the attention of the student culture. The latest product, "Life 101: Learning To Say 'YES' to Life!" is a two-part video designed for the public school. Part one was purposely made for general assemblies and describes the problem of teenage suicide. Part two, to be shown outside of class time, gives the ultimate answer in Jesus Christ. For a list of publications offered by Shepherd, locate the order form found in the back of this book.

- **Student Conferences** — The backbone of Shepherd is the weekend conferences held in the larger cities of the nation. With the ministry of music and praise from Todd Proctor, Al Holley and others, and the teaching of Dawson McAllister, students eagerly attend these memorable events. This past year over 82,000 students attended these weekend events.

- **Youth Minister Conference** — A weeklong conference presently held during the fall in Dallas, this event is designed to minister to the youth pastor or worker and spouse. "Youth Ministry" is a joint venture of Shepherd Ministries and Rapha, and seeks to encourage, challenge, and assist youth ministers and their spouses.

- **Parent Seminar** — "Preparing Your Teenager for Sexuality" video seminar. Available to churches as a one-day event, Dawson teaches this seminar via giant screen video. Aaron Shook, a Christian singer/songwriter, leads the seminar and provides live music. This seminar equips parents with a step-by-step method for teaching kids God's view of sex. "Preparing Your Teenager for Sexuality" is also available as a stand-alone video series.

- **Television** — Dawson McAllister's mission is to reach the American student. Though many will not darken the door of a church, all of them will turn the dial of a television. A series of three prime-time tv specials were produced and aired in 22 of the largest cities in America to reach those students. In Dallas in 1989 the program, "Too Young To Die" took first place in the Neilsen ratings for that evening hour.

- **Radio** — The newest tool to reach the American teenager is live call-in radio entitled, "Dawson McAllister Live." This one-hour weekly satellite program brings troubled, confused teenagers into contact with straight talk and clear Biblical guidance. Each student who calls and receives Dawson's compassionate counsel on the air represents thousands of others with similar problems. Not only do they hear Dawson's advice, but the students are invited to call for one-on-one counseling on a toll-free line.

More from Dawson McAllister and Shepherd Ministries...

STUDENT MANUALS FROM DAWSON

A Walk With Christ To The Cross
A Walk With Christ Through The Resurrection
A Walk With Christ Through Eternity
Discussion Manual for Student Discipleship Vols. I,II
Discussion Manual for Student Relationships Vols. I,II,III
Finding Hope For Your Home
Making Peace At Home
Pack Your Bags—Jesus Is Coming
Search For Significance
Student Conference Follow-up Manual
The Great War
Who Are You, God?
Who Are You, Jesus?
You, God, and Your Sexuality

TEACHER MANUALS FROM DAWSON

A Walk With Christ To The Cross
A Walk With Christ Through Eternity
Discussion Manual for Student Relationships Vols. I,II,III
Finding Hope For Your Home
Making Peace At Home
Pack Your Bags—Jesus Is Coming
Preparing Your Teenager For Sexuality
The Great War
Who Are You, God?
Who Are You, Jesus?

TEACHING KITS FROM DAWSON

A Walk With Christ Through Eternity
Finding Hope For Your Home
Making Peace At Home
Pack Your Bags—Jesus Is Coming

BOOKS FROM DAWSON

How To Know If You're Really In Love
Please Don't Tell My Parents—Answers For Kids In Crises

VIDEOS FROM DAWSON

A Walk With Christ To The Cross
Been There...Made That (Jesus Is God)
Been There...Done That (Jesus Is Man)
Life 101—Learning To Say Yes! To Life
Preparing Your Teenager For Sexuality
When Tragedy Strikes
Why R.U.?—The Why and Way Out of Substance Abuse

MUSIC FROM SHEPHERD

Inside Your Love—Chris Tomlin
Live The Difference—Todd Proctor
Live The Difference Praise and Worship Kit—Todd Proctor
Never The Same—Todd Proctor
180—Todd Proctor
Power Up: Praise For Youth—Todd Proctor
Power Up: Praise and Worship Kit—Todd Proctor
Road of Eternity—Todd Proctor and Joel Engle
The Forever Praise Project—Todd Proctor and Joel Engle
The Forever Praise Project Praise and Worship Kit
—Todd Proctor and Joel Engle
We Stand As One—Todd Proctor
We Stand As One Praise and Worship Kit—Todd Proctor

OTHER SHEPHERD MINISTRIES RESOURCES

Live On Location In the Book Of Proverbs—Mark Matlock
The Search For Significance—Robert McGee
Youth Worker's Fun Kit, Vol. 1—Mark Matlock

....

_____ YES! Please send me a <u>FREE</u> copy of your latest product catalog.

☐ STUDENT ☐ ADULT

Name _____

Church _____

Street Address _____

City/State/Zip _____

Phone Number _____

For More Information Or To Order
Any Of These Products Contact:
Shepherd Ministries
2221 Walnut Hill Lane
Irving, TX 75038
(972) 580-8000
Fax (972) 580-1FAX